INSIDE:
WOMEN BEHIND BARS

Also by Emma French & Jonathan Levi:

Inside Broadmoor
Inside Wakefield Prison
Inside Belmarsh

INSIDE:
WOMEN BEHIND BARS

Behind Closed Doors of Notorious Women's Prisons

EMMA FRENCH & JONATHAN LEVI

First published in the UK in 2026 by Blink Publishing
An imprint of Bonnier Books UK
5th Floor, HYLO, 105 Bunhill Row,
London, EC1Y 8LZ

A CIP catalogue record for this book is available from the British Library.

Paperback ISBN: 978-1-78870-975-0

Also available as an ebook and an audiobook

1 3 5 7 9 10 8 6 4 2

Design and Typeset by Envy Design Ltd
Printed and bound in Great Britain by CPI (UK) Ltd, Croydon CR0 4YY

At Bonnier Books UK, we are committed to publishing sustainably.
Find out more here: bonnierbooks.co.uk/sustainability

Every reasonable effort has been made to trace copyright holders of material reproduced in this book, but if any have been inadvertently overlooked the publishers would be glad to hear from them.

The authorised representative in the EEA is
Bonnier Books UK (Ireland) Limited.
Registered office address:
Block B, The Crescent Building
Northwood, Santry
Dublin 9, D09 C6X8
Ireland
compliance@bonnierbooks.ie

www.bonnierbooks.co.uk

*'I want to give you a bit of advice. If you end up with
a bad man, then run away from that man and run to
the police. Wherever you're going, whatever you do,
I hope you don't come back here.'*
ROSE WEST TO ELEANOR BROWN ON THE EVE OF
HER DEPARTURE FROM NEW HALL

Contents

Prologue

There would be plenty of time for questions later. Right now, a riot was under way.

Officer Kay Lumb was suddenly in the thick of it. The female wing at Risley Remand Centre had been building towards it all day, but thanks to one notorious inmate, the simmering tension had somehow reached boiling point without anyone noticing.

New Hall took a lot of the remand from Risley, which is where I first met Gillian. She was an absolute bully. Straight away we didn't get on.

I was tipped off that Gillian had made a knife, once, too. She had got a piece of wooden handle off a gardening tool and had strapped the handle of the knife with something like a leather shoelace. She had a gripe with an officer, and she didn't want to lose face. The last thing any prisoner wants is to be known as a grass, so the prisoner who told me was careful. 'I'm just going off the wing for a second,' she said. 'There's a knife in the bed on the wing; it's meant for . . .' and she named a certain officer.

Gillian started the riot on the female wing at Risley.

Normally a prisoner will tip you off. Not this time. Gillian even intimidated a lot of staff. She did weights at the gym and there was a silent agreement among officers because she wanted to come to the gym. She bullied people to bring drugs in. She was taking their visiting orders. She would only go for the weak prisoners.

At Risley there were two dining rooms: 26-foot rooms with probably about 40 prisoners in each dining room. One with the serving hatch and one had the TV in. Meals were normally silent. I wasn't on the wing when the riot kicked off.

There were knives and all sorts behind the serving hatch. There were alarm bells on the female wing that connected to the male wing. I got a call on the radio saying there was an alarm on the female wing. It was crazy. Nobody noticed the inmates hadn't eaten their meals. They hadn't smashed the telly, but they had left bits of their meals on the floor, so we were all slipping over everywhere.

I shouted, 'Get the hatches down!' but they didn't do it fast enough. I jumped on to where the food comes up in a hot trolley and you slide big containers on to a heated area and I pulled the two shutters down and locked the door to the first room where they were chanting and carrying on.

We went in to break it up. Gillian was first through the door. She walked past me and I looked at her. We had to go in as teams with shields. We cleared the other dining room *first – we had the extra staff from the landings. Gillian, as the ringleader, was put in a room on the hospital wing. She tried to refuse. We said, 'Gill, you will either go on your own two feet or we are taking you.'*

Gillian was seeing another prisoner, a pharmacist that had started selling drugs. She was terrified of Gillian, and she walked her to the hospital wing. She could hardly talk. She just had a little croak left.

I said to the staff there, 'You need to deal with her.' They said, 'You're going on E1.' It was a tiny unit, a big cell divided into two called a strip cell. She knew that was the punishment block. So they put her in the 'silent cell' on the hospital wing. In those days prisoners could lose time. The Governor could give them extra time without going to court. She served an extra 28 days. The whole prison was locked up for a few days.

Gillian had organised it all.

What was Gillian's motivation? Probably down to lack of family. Risley was very basic and quite strict. They got what they were entitled to. They have shut that female wing now . . .

MAJOR CONTRIBUTORS

The women's estate differs in so many ways from the male estate: more intimate, more complex in its social dynamics, a world in which 80 per cent of the population are victims of domestic abuse and well over half are separated from children they left outside. Of those who contributed to this book – as former officers, governors, prisoners and professionals – many requested varying degrees of anonymity. We have respected every level of privacy asked of us, and that respect has allowed us to include far more than we otherwise could have done. There are many more voices in these pages than the names listed below.

Anastasia Severn

Anastasia has a successful sales career now and a lively social media presence @adhdqueen7 and as Diamond in the Rough. During her time in the secure estate she shared a unit with Lorraine Thorpe, the youngest convicted female double murderer in British criminal history, and went on to do time at HMP Eastwood Park, HMP New Hall and HMP Drake Hall. She has spoken about her experiences to raise awareness of mental health, grooming, gangs and drugs – in her words, 'to help the youth of today not make the same mistakes'.

Bev Butler

Bev joined the Prison Service in 1987. She arrived at HMP New Hall that summer almost by accident – and found herself part of the founding cohort of a women's prison with more staff than inmates. She spent much of the next two decades in the service, and remains in close contact with colleagues from a career that shaped her as much as she shaped the place.

Cath Thompson

Cath joined the Prison Service in 1985 at the age of 22 – an age she now regards as too young. At Leeds she became the first female officer on the landings to become pregnant, navigating that distinction with the same matter-of-fact good humour and professionalism she brought to everything else. She worked in segregation, on court escorts and on the wings across both the women's and male estate.

Dainya Ebanks

Dainya now works in two roles connected to the criminal justice system and is developing an advocacy platform under the name 'Thank God I Went to Prison', aimed at raising awareness of grooming among young teenagers. She served her time at HMP Holloway and Bronzefield, having been convicted as a teenager, and for the better part of a decade kept her experience buried – swept to the back of her mind, she says, as though it had not happened. Speaking about it openly is recent work for her.

Debbie James

Debbie has retired from the Prison Service and now runs her own jewellery business. She began her career at Bullwood Hall in Essex before a brief period on escort duty at Brixton and then HMP New Hall, where she spent most of her service. She also worked on the mother and baby unit for several years and conducted hundreds of court and hospital escorts, including a visit to Cookham Wood during which she came face to face with Myra Hindley.

Eleanor Brown

Eleanor is a former prisoner at HMP New Hall who speaks with frankness about her experience of the women's estate. She spent periods of time at open prison including Askham Grange, and towards the end of her sentence was housed on Rivendell – the enhanced and restricted status wing at New Hall – three doors along from Rosemary West. She had not anticipated the conversation that took place the night before her release.

Jo Taylor

A former officer for 15 years, serving at both HMP New Hall and Wakefield, Jo has seen things that would make most people's hair stand on end – which is perhaps why she left to become a highly successful and prize-winning specialist in bespoke scalp micropigmentation. She is also a Royalist superfan and star of Jonathan's hit TV series, *Lip-Reading the Royals*.

Juli Flintoff

Juli joined New Hall in September 1997, one week into her marriage and having cut her honeymoon short she was posted directly to the lifers' wing. She went on to become a drug dog handler, a mandatory drug-testing officer and a winner of a national supervisory management award. She has written four books, including *The Secret Back Door* and *The Daisy Chain*, and retains a detailed and often unsettling knowledge of what the female estate does to the women it holds and the people who try to care for them.

Kay Lumb

Kay joined the Prison Service in 1977 and was medically retired in 2002, after approximately 25 years' service, in which she worked as a PE instructor, a landing officer, a control room and surveillance instructor. She also experienced being the person escorting Beverley Allitt to hospital. She began her career at Drake Hall open prison before transferring to Risley Remand Centre – where a riot started as described in this book's prologue – and later to HMP New Hall when it opened.

Neah Tuohy

Witty and articulate, Neah spent a decade across most of England's women's prisons. She served the final two years during the Covid pandemic, emerged to run her own company in youth advocacy, and now uses everything she knows. 'If you're not going to make some noise for the people who can't be heard, then what was it for?'

Nicola Webster

Nicola arrived at HMP New Hall via a nursing agency and a career in the British Army. She worked there for approximately ten years, qualifying as both a general nurse and a mental health nurse while in post, before eventually becoming matron. She encountered women in vulnerable and sometimes extraordinary circumstances. She now works as a nurse practitioner with her own clinics.

Saj Zafar

Saj made history when, at the age of 24, she became the first and youngest Asian Muslim woman to be appointed as a prison governor in the United Kingdom. Her career in criminal justice began at Feltham Young Offenders Institution, where she established the country's first specialist therapeutic unit for young sex offenders. She is the CEO and founder of the Institute for Change and the LeadHERship Academy.

Simon Peters

Simon Peters currently works in the justice sector in an Employee Relations role and has vast experience of prisons, since joining HMP Feltham back in 1999, which he conveys with intelligence and compassion. At Holloway, where he worked until its closure in 2016, he implemented safer cells, ran the segregation unit and was also in charge of the reception area. He was the Chairman of the Holloway branch of the Prison Officers' Association for 11 years and developed a reputation – among staff and prisoners alike – for getting things done by the straightforwardly radical method of keeping his word. His formula for the work: firm, fair, human.

Stephen Hillis

Stephen is Deputy Head of NI Prison Programmes for North West Regional College. He has an interesting pedigree in the field: his grandfather was a prison officer at Crumlin Road Gaol in Belfast and was present at the last hanging there, and his uncle was a prison officer at Wandsworth. His view of what success looks like is precise: the best outcome is when the individuals you have worked with don't return to prison.

Suzy Dymond-White

Suzy is a warm, humane and thoughtful former prison governor who now chairs three charity boards. She joined the Prison Service in 1987 as an officer at HMP Holloway and was among the first women deployed on male landings under cross-sex deployment rules. During her career she held approximately 20 roles across both estates, governed three prisons, and at HMP Eastwood Park, where she served until her retirement, held the national portfolio for health and wellbeing in women's prisons.

Tracy Mackness

Charismatic and entrepreneurial, Tracy is the founder of The Giggly Pig Company, an Essex-based business specialising in handmade sausages. She lives on her farm with approximately 800 pigs. She started with just 30, purchased a week after her release. She served five and a half years of a ten-year sentence, fell in love with a Saddleback pig named Biddy, and won the Gold Award at the 2007 Barclays Trading Places Awards.

Wendy Sinclair-Gieben

Wendy is a former HM Chief Inspector of Prisons for Scotland, a role in which she successfully campaigned for legislation to remove all children from the Scottish prison estate – a battle she describes as the one she fought hardest and is most glad she won. She began her career as a prison teacher before fast-tracking through the direct entry scheme, going on to hold posts at HMP Nottingham, HMP Ashfield and HMP Kilmarnock, as well as two establishments in Western Australia. She has led inspections of HMP Stirling and both Community Custody Units in Scotland.

Yvonne Simpson

Yvonne is a hairdresser and salon owner who co-manages her business with her family and is completing a degree in psychology and criminology while working pro bono to support women leaving the criminal justice system. She served 11 months across HMP Styal, HMP Peterborough and Askham Grange open prison, entering Styal seven months pregnant. She gave birth to Jadine while in custody at Peterborough, spent part of her sentence on the mother and baby unit with two babies, and was released from Askham Grange with a double pushchair, all her belongings piled on top of it, and no one there to collect her.

Chapter I

Introduction

*'People only regret what they've done when the door
shuts behind them.'*
SIMON PETERS

Women's prisons are in crisis.

On the morning of her 18th birthday, Neah Tuohy transferred from a juvenile detention unit to an adult female prison with fake tan still on her legs. In the bag they had taken from her at reception was a bottle of champagne for her birthday celebration planned for that evening. She had not washed the tan off because she had assumed she would be home to do it. 'So when I got to prison the next morning, I hadn't washed it off, and it goes really orange if you don't wash it off. So then I'm there looking like this – and I thought, "Oh, my God, I wish I had a tracksuit."' She could hear shouting from every direction as she was brought through – '"Yo, new gal, where you from?"' She had to be the youngest woman in the women's estate in England that day. She was 18 years old and eight hours into being an adult. She was a sitting target, and she knew it.

She would spend the next ten years inside.

Anastasia Severn was 16 when the van came for her. It was small, with blacked-out windows. They gave her a sandwich and crisps on the way. 'Obviously, I didn't want to eat because I was just in shock. I didn't think I was going to jail, to be honest.' Her mother was a police officer. Her father was a plumber. She had been, she said, easily led. When she arrived at Rainsbrook Secure Training Centre it was late and everyone was locked in. She lay in her cell listening to the fan and when she woke up she had one thought: 'I'm still here.'

She would spend the next five years moving between Rainsbrook, Eastwood Park, New Hall and Drake Hall. Rainsbrook closed in 2023. By the time she left she had turned 21 inside, shared landings with some of the most notorious women in the British penal system, nearly broken a woman's neck in an industrial tumble dryer she herself had switched on, counted plastic gloves for eight hours a day for five months, been assaulted in communal showers and woken in the night to find a stranger standing over her. She walked out in the clothes she was wearing, having given everything she owned to the women who remained.

The women's estate holds fewer than one in 20 of all prisoners in England and Wales, yet accounts for more than a quarter of all self-harm incidents behind bars. As of 2024, 3,635 women were held in custody against 87,869 men. More than half of all sentences handed to women are for less than six months. More than a third of those are for shoplifting. Nearly two-thirds of women entering custody have experienced domestic abuse. These are not, for the most part, dangerous criminals. They are, in the main, deeply damaged ones.

They are also statistically almost invisible against the cases that make the headlines: the whole-life tariffs, the names that have not left us.

What the officers found on the landings, despite the training, could come as an equal shock to the prisoners' experiences. Men will tell you if they have an issue with you, Cath Thompson told us. 'But the women – they don't. They bottle it up. They bottle it up and they bottle it up, and then it comes out in a cut-up, a set fire, a barricade, a flooding, an assault. You never know with women what's coming round next.'

This level of underlying trauma is one the system can be unequipped to address. 'Most of our women, as you probably know better than me, are victims themselves,' said Stephen Hillis. 'There's no doubt about it.' Nicola Webster estimated that potentially 95 per cent of the population she worked with was on a detox on arrival. What came through the gate alongside them was a level of need that left clinical staff at a loss. 'A lot of it would be containing women with acute psychiatric problems that there were no beds for in the community,' she said. 'You're just containing people, which ethically and morally isn't right, is it?' The result, as Simon Peters saw it, was a system so broken that incarceration had become its own form of relief. 'For some women, prison was a period of respite,' he said. 'That is an uncomfortable thing to say, because prison should not be the safer option, it's upside down. But I saw women who were exhausted by abuse, addiction, debt, coercion and violence. For them, custody could become a pause in the cycle, even though it was never the answer to what had brought them there.' They would withdraw from substances, put weight on, get treatment for their various ailments and just at the point that they would start to reintegrate into what society would deem as normal, they would be released to start the entire cycle again. The public know this as the 'revolving door' part of the justice system.

Even Wendy Sinclair-Gieben, who governed prisons on two continents, admitted: 'I prefer managing men. Because it's simpler, it's much, much simpler. I tended to get wrapped up in the women and get distressed by them.' Juli Flintoff understood why: 'You've got four, five hundred women that at some point are premenstrual, that argue and fight like ball-street fighting on the yard. And they're concerned about their homes. Concerned if the kids are all right. If somebody's paying the bills. Is their partner having it away with somebody else. So they're so stressed.'

Juli ran the drug dogs at New Hall. 'I always used to think, by the grace of God go I,' she told us. 'Women's prison is a very dark place. Not much light coming through the bars.'

To all of them: this book belongs to you as much as it belongs to us.

Now it's time to take you inside.

UK Women's Prisons: A History & the Estate Today

'If you close Eastwood Park and you live in West Cornwall and you get sent to prison, you're probably going to go to Derbyshire. Some of the women don't even know where that is.'

SUZY DYMOND-WHITE

The geography of women's imprisonment in England and Wales tells you almost everything you need to know about how the system was built: not for the women inside it, not for the communities they come from, and not for the possibility of return.

There are currently 124 prisons in England and Wales. One hundred and eight are run by His Majesty's Prison and Probation Service; 16 are privately managed by companies including G4S, Serco and Sodexo. Within that system, women represent just 4 per cent of the total prison population. They are an afterthought in the architecture of British justice, and they have been since the beginning.

Victorian prisons originally held men, women and children together in conditions that were damp, insanitary and overcrowded, with petty offenders sharing space with serious criminals, debtors and those awaiting trial. Women who had broken the law were understood as a particular category of problem: not merely criminal but deviant in a more fundamental sense, having transgressed not just legal but social and moral boundaries. Female criminals were seen as demons in the jailhouse, a disruptive force requiring a different kind of management. Activities were geared towards preparing women for life outside prison by training them in what the authorities considered their natural role: domestic service. Idleness was seen as one of the causes of female criminality. Work – the right kind of work – was seen as the cure.

Reformatories aimed to legislate morality through criminalising female sexuality. The women inside them were defined more by the anxieties of those who ran them than by any coherent understanding of what had brought them there.

Between 1853 and 1869 alone, 70 women were removed from female convict prisons and placed in lunatic asylums – a figure that tells you something about the extent to which mental illness and criminality were conflated, and about how the system dealt with women it could not easily classify.

By the time Bev Butler joined the Prison Service in 1987, some things had changed and others had not. She was part of the founding cohort at HMP New Hall, arriving in the summer of that year when the prison was in the early stages of its conversion from a young offenders' detention centre to a women's establishment. She remembers what the female estate looked like in those early years.

'I joined the service on 5 May 1987,' Bev told us. 'I went to Low Newton first to have a look round and see if that's what I wanted to do. And then down to Newbold Revel to do my training. I remember my first day going into Durham because, as you know, male prisons are categorised and females aren't. And so when we went in, it was all gated. It was the female estate there. Didn't hold many prisoners, only about ten or 12. It was a prison within the prison, and they said no, it wasn't meant for the men. So they stuck the women in it. When we got to New Hall there was a chief officer there, a fellow called Ray Andrews – a lovely man, died now. He was recruiting. I lived in Lincoln at the time. The only prison there was a male prison at Lincoln. And to be honest, I wanted to get out of the city. There were probably eight or nine of us who all started at New Hall on the same day.'

The detail is telling. A women's prison with ten or 12 inmates, set inside a men's institution not built for them. Staff recruited almost by accident, by a man who happened to be in the right room at the right time.

Suzy Dymond-White joined the Prison Service the same year, as an officer at HMP Holloway. Over a decades-long career that would take her from junior officer to governing governor of three prisons, she came to know the female estate from every angle. Her account of those first years illustrates how fundamentally the service was built around assumptions that had little to do with women.

In the 1980s, she explained, there was no question of choosing where you would work or even what kind of prison you would enter. It was the Women's Prison Service, and women who joined it were posted wherever the service required them. 'You don't choose Holloway – you didn't choose where you went,' she told us. 'You joined the Women's Prison Service, you were told where to turn up for your induction – which in my case was Holloway – you then went away to training school, and at about the end of week seven you got a little brown envelope that said where you were going. It's not like it is now where you apply to work in a prison. You joined the service and it was a bit like joining the army – you waited for your posting. And then everybody scrambled around with their brown envelopes, seeing if they could swap with people to get nearer home or do something different.'

Suzy's first proper posting was East Sutton Park in Kent, around the time of the 1987 Fresh Start initiative, which had abolished overtime and increased staffing levels across the estate, forcing some prisons to take on new staff for the first time in years. The posting took her from Holloway's remand population to something almost unrecognisable. 'East Sutton Park was 90-something women, right out in the country,' she said. 'Open prison. Most women working either within the prison or in the big walled gardens – they were providing floral displays for offices in London, they had big greenhouses producing vegetables, they had a farm with pigs, and you could walk around the lake. I remember cycling around the lanes with four women as they were training for the local half marathon, or getting them used to going shopping again, or they were going to get a job in Maidstone, so you'd take them into Maidstone and say, "Let's just walk up the high street; there's the bus stop." Worlds apart, those two places; absolutely worlds apart.'

As much as she valued East Sutton Park, and could see the benefits for the inmates too, she had recognised early that it was not where a long career would be forged. 'I felt that if I was going to prepare myself for a long career, it was not the place to be. I needed to be at the tougher end of this if I was going to properly prepare myself.' A chance swap with a colleague posted to Pucklechurch near Bristol – a women's remand unit run within a mixed establishment – gave her what she needed. It was fast-paced and, she said, you saw everything you were ever going to see in prison life within months of arriving.

The 1990 riots, which began at Strangeways in April of that year and spread through the estate, brought the women's remand unit at Pucklechurch to an abrupt end. 'We had the riots,' she told us. 'We lost our unit. They closed it because there was so much damage following the riots. I lived through that time, where the place was absolutely just annihilated, and they closed the women's remand unit, and we were offered – you know, what do you want to do, where do you want to go? And cross-sex deployment had come in at that point. So I went to Dartmoor.'

The contrast between Dartmoor and any women's prison she had worked in was the sharpest she had encountered. 'Dartmoor was Category B, and they were all long-term, all serving very long sentences, and they all just went there to get their heads down and work,' she said. 'That's the marked difference between what I knew as male convicted prisons and women's prisons, which pretty much always had a remand function. The men were quite happy just to get their heads down. They didn't need that constant engagement like the women need.' We asked her to say more precisely what that difference looked like in practice. 'You couldn't have a wing of a thousand women, because you'd just never achieve anything,' she said. 'They just respond so much better to small units. Two hundred and fifty or three hundred men on a wing, and you shout right, goodnight, it's eight o'clock, and you'd hear the doors go bang, bang, bang. You have 50 women on a unit and you shout goodnight, and they're all going, oh, I just – I haven't got my water yet. Oh, I need to talk to you about that. It's just like a different world managing those two kinds of people. The women need constant communication, engagement, almost affirmation that they're there, and they're okay, and it's okay.'

The prison estate today consists of 12 women's prisons in England. There are none in Wales. Women from Welsh courts are sent across the border, a geographical reality that creates particular difficulties around maintaining contact with children and families, and a structural contradiction in terms of healthcare: NHS England holds responsibility for healthcare in women's prisons, while women returning to Wales must be handed back to Welsh health and social care systems, a transition that has long been acknowledged to require significant improvement. Welsh reform campaigners and the Welsh government have raised the absence of any custodial facility on Welsh soil as a persistent concern; for the women affected by it, the consequences are immediate and concrete.

Security categorisation for women operates differently from the male estate. Women are classified into four categories: Restricted Status, the equivalent of Category A for men and rarely applied given the relatively low number of women convicted of offences serious enough to require it; Closed, for those whom escape must be made very difficult; Semi-open, which was phased out in 2009; and Open, for those who can be safely trusted to remain within the prison boundaries. Currently only three establishments house the highest-risk female prisoners: HMP Low Newton, HMP New Hall and HMP Bronzefield.

The custodial consequences for women are disproportionate in ways that are not always visible in raw sentencing data. A six-month sentence for a man might mean a disruption to his life. The same sentence for a woman who is the primary carer for children may mean those children are taken into care, the family home is lost, and employment ends. The physical distance of the estate from the communities these women come from compounds everything. As Suzy puts it: if the nearest women's prison to where you live is 200 miles away, your family may simply not come.

What follows is an account of each of the establishments in the current women's estate – their histories, their particular characters, and some of the notable prisoners they have held. Three of them – HMP Peterborough, HMP Bronzefield and HMP New Hall – are the subject of separate chapters later in this book.

Beginning in the North, HMP Low Newton sits in Brasside, County Durham. Its setting nestled in among housing, with children playing right outside, makes it feel oddly homely. The notorious HMP Frankland, one of the country's highest security men's prisons, hunches next to it, crackling with menace and lacking any of the strange suburban domesticity of Low Newton's immediate surroundings. Originally built in 1965 as a mixed remand centre accommodating 65 males and 11 females, Low Newton was redesignated in September 1998 as an all-female prison following a substantial refurbishment programme. Since that redesignation it has served as the primary high-security custodial facility for women in the north of England, receiving female prisoners from courts across the region and holding a significant proportion of women serving life sentences or very long determinate terms. The prison has a capacity of around 340. One wing accommodates long-term and restricted status prisoners. Another operates as a drug-free unit. Perhaps the most significant specialist provision at Low

Newton is the Primrose Project, the only unit within the women's prison estate specifically designed to treat women with dangerous and severe personality disorders.

Low Newton has housed some of the most notorious women in British criminal history. Rosemary West served part of her whole-life sentence at Low Newton before transferring to HMP New Hall in 2019. Joanna Dennehy – convicted in 2013 of murdering three men in and around Peterborough in a spree lasting ten days and subsequently attacking two more victims in Herefordshire – is one of only three women in England and Wales currently subject to a whole-life order. Lucy Letby, the neonatal nurse convicted of murdering seven babies and attempting to murder six more at the Countess of Chester Hospital at her original 2023 trial, with a further attempted-murder conviction following a 2024 retrial, was sentenced to a whole-life order. She has been held at HMP New Hall, HMP Low Newton and HMP Bronzefield since her conviction. Beinash Batool received life with a minimum term in December 2024 for her part in the horrific murder of Sara Sharif, not a whole-life order. She is also in Bronzefield.

Moving into the North West, HMP Styal occupies one of the more unusual settings of any prison in England. Located in the village of Styal in Cheshire, it takes up the former buildings of the Styal Cottage Homes, a Victorian orphanage for destitute children from the Manchester area that opened in 1898 and closed in 1956. The site became a women's prison in 1962, when women were transferred from HMP Manchester. From 1983 it began holding young offenders, and in 1999 a new wing was added to accommodate unsentenced women following the closure of the Risley remand centre, increasing the prison's size by 60 per cent.

Styal has a troubled history and was the most difficult environment that several of our contributors encountered. In 2003 it was singled out by the Howard League for Penal Reform as having one of the worst suicide records in England and Wales, with bullying, drugs and overcrowding identified as likely contributing factors. The BBC documentary *Women on the Edge*, broadcast in February 2006, brought conditions at Styal to wider public attention. A 2018 inspection found self-harm remained high but concentrated in a small number of women, and praised resettlement strategies and race relations. Now, Styal holds a mother and baby unit for children up to 18 months and operates a Clink restaurant open to the public, housed in what was formerly the prison chapel.

Crossing into the East Midlands, HMP Foston Hall is located in the village of Foston in Derbyshire, within a Grade II listed Jacobean mansion house built in 1863 and acquired by the Prison Service in 1953. It reopened on 31 July 1997 as a closed women's prison following substantial refurbishment, and operates as a local resettlement prison serving courts across the Midlands, with a capacity of just over 300. Foston Hall's recent inspection record has been problematic. An unannounced inspection in October and November 2021 awarded the prison the lowest possible rating for safety – the first time that had occurred anywhere in the women's estate since the Inspectorate developed its current framework. Inspectors found self-harm at the highest level across the entire female estate, two women having taken their own lives since the previous inspection. A further unannounced inspection in January 2025 found that although violence was rarely serious and assaults on staff were falling, the overall number of violent incidents remained the highest in the estate. Karen Matthews was held at Foston Hall before her release in April 2012.

A short distance away in Staffordshire, HMP Drake Hall is located near Eccleshall. The site was originally built to house female munitions workers during the Second World War, then later operated as a teacher training college before the Prison Service took it over in the 1960s as a men's open prison. In 1974 it was converted to a women's prison, a designation it has held ever since, and it holds around 315 adult and young adult women. Unlike most closed prisons, Drake Hall operates an unusually relaxed internal regime, somewhat retaining that open prison vibe. Prisoners are never locked in their rooms during the day and have free movement around the site during daylight hours. At night they are locked only into their house blocks, not individual cells.

Anastasia served time at Drake Hall and described its character as something she had not anticipated. The houses were named after towns across England – Bristol, Margate, Ipswich, Norwich – and the Tannoy system called each house in turn for meals rather than locking women away for them. She worked first in waste management, collecting and sorting bins across the site, then found her way to the hair salon. 'It actually felt like a workplace,' she told us. 'There were no bars on the windows. It felt like a proper salon. So I didn't feel like I was in jail for most of the day.' The communal showers and toilets – separate from cells, shared within each house block – were one of the features that set Drake Hall apart from any closed establishment she had known.

Further south in South Gloucestershire, HMP Eastwood Park is located in Falfield and opened as a women's prison in March 1996, receiving staff and prisoners from the former HMP Pucklechurch. It holds women aged 18 and over, with a capacity of approximately 377 and a mother and baby unit. In May 2016, Jessica Whitchurch died in the prison after fellow prisoners had bullied and goaded her into taking her own life; prison officers failed to challenge the bullying. An unannounced inspection in June and July 2025 found that although leadership had improved some areas, self-harm, violence and use of force had all increased since the previous inspection and were among the highest in the country, and women with severe mental health conditions were waiting far too long for transfer to secure hospitals.

Suzy served as governor of Eastwood Park until her retirement. It was where she ended a career that had taken her from a junior officer posting at HMP Holloway in 1987, through Pucklechurch, Dartmoor, Coldingley,

Winchester and three governing roles, to the most senior operational position in the female estate. She described one of the central absurdities of the system in a single observation: if Eastwood Park closed, the nearest prison for a woman from West Cornwall might be in Derbyshire. A distance like that does not just separate a woman from her family. It makes the relationship between custody and rehabilitation – between punishment and any realistic prospect of change – almost impossible to sustain.

Anastasia also spent time at Eastwood Park, having been transferred there from Rainsbrook Secure Centre, and found herself on the juvenile wing before her 18th birthday moved her across to the adult estate. E Wing, the main receiving wing, held 200 women or more across double and single cells. Workshop 5, where she spent several months counting plastic gloves into bags for eight hours a day, is a memory she returned to with something close to horror. 'Honestly, I ended up going mad in the end,' she told us, 'and got put into hairdressing.' She left Eastwood Park with a level two hairdressing qualification and went into the trade on the outside.

Next, our tour moves east into Surrey, where two very different establishments sit within a relatively short distance of one another. HMP Send occupies the former site of a smallpox isolation hospital near Woking, rebuilt entirely as a women's prison in 1999. It is managed by HMPS with an operational capacity of around 255 and holds a high proportion of women serving life sentences or long determinate terms. Send operates several specialist units, including a 40-bed Psychologically Informed Planned Environment unit – known as PIPE – providing therapeutic support for women with complex psychological needs. A 2025 inspection found Send to be a very good, well-led prison. Notable prisoners held there include Jane Andrews, formerly a dresser to Sarah, Duchess of York, convicted in 2001 of murdering her partner, Thomas Cressman, and Vanessa George, a Plymouth nursery worker convicted in 2009 of sexually abusing children in her care as part of an online paedophile network.

Also in Surrey, HMP Downview is located in the Sutton area. It opened in 1989 as a Category C male prison and was converted to a women's establishment in September 2001. It closed in 2014 and reopened in 2016 when HMP Holloway closed, absorbing a large number of Holloway's prisoners. Its operational capacity is 356, including 16 dedicated places on E Wing, opened in March 2019 as the United Kingdom's first dedicated unit for transgender women prisoners. The unit was created following a 2018 policy review prompted by high-profile incidents, including the assault by transgender prisoner Karen White on two women at HMP New Hall. E Wing is a stand-alone 16-bed unit, physically separate from the main female population, accessible only under supervision following risk assessment. In November 2025, an adjournment debate heard arguments that the arrangement violated both the 1823 Gaols Act and the April 2025 Supreme Court ruling that single-sex provision must be based on biological sex.

Government ministers stated that there had been no recorded assault by a transgender prisoner in the women's estate since 2019.

The estate is completed by two open prisons – HMP Askham Grange in North Yorkshire and HMP East Sutton Park in Kent – which form a category all of their own within the female estate and are examined in detail in Chapter 20.

There is also the question of young girls. Women's prisons in England and Wales mix adults with juveniles in ways that have no equivalent in the male estate, where young offenders are separated. The implications of this are something Neah, who first entered the system as a teenager and spent a decade passing through eight women's establishments, described with the clarity of direct experience. She told us that some prisons made more effort than others to separate younger women from the general population – Holloway, she said, could manage it to a degree – but that across most of the estate, the mixing was a fact of life. Women, she said, wanted an easy sentence. They brushed things off. The result was an environment in which young women learned to navigate adult prison culture from their first day, with very little institutional protection from what that culture contained.

It comes down to what each individual institution decides to believe about the women inside it. The evidence from the establishments described in this chapter suggests that belief, even now, is far from consistent – and that for too many of those women, it falls a very long way short.

The oldest of those institutions, and the most layered in its history, was HMP Holloway. What happened there over 160 years is where this book turns next.

CHAPTER 3

HMP Holloway

'Knowledge is currency, knowledge is power, always.'
SIMON PETERS

Oddly, the most notorious women's prison, the one that almost everyone outside the service is the first to name, no longer has women in its cells. It has also, bizarrely, left inner London without a women's prison.

There was a moment during Simon Peters' first tour of Holloway, before he had even agreed to transfer there from Feltham, when he understood something about the place that would take years to fully articulate. Walking from A Block through corridors that seemed to swallow sound, not seeing a single prisoner, hearing only moaning and calling from behind wooden doors – wooden doors, in a prison this size – he thought he had arrived somewhere under extraordinary pressure.

It had not always looked like that.

HMP Holloway opened in 1852 as a mixed-sex prison on the northern edge of what was then a fast-expanding London. As demand for space for female prisoners grew, driven in part by the closure of Newgate, it was redesignated as female-only in 1903, becoming the first prison of its kind in the country and one of the largest in Europe. It would remain so for more than a century, accumulating history in layers: suffragettes, political internees, notorious killers, and in its final years some of the most damaged women in the criminal justice system. It closed in July 2016.

Before the First World War, Holloway held those suffragettes who were arrested for breaking the law in the campaign for women's suffrage. Emmeline Pankhurst, Emily Davison, Constance Markievicz, Charlotte Despard, Mary Richardson and Ethel Smyth were among those imprisoned there. The cells they occupied gave Holloway a unique and lasting place in the history of women's rights in this country. During the Second World War, it housed individuals detained under Defence Regulation 18B, including Diana Mitford and her husband Sir Oswald Mosley, who were permitted to share a cottage within the prison grounds.

Ruth Ellis was the last woman to be executed in Britain. In April 1955, she shot her lover David Blakely outside the Magdala pub in South Hill Park, Hampstead, following a turbulent relationship defined by violence and control. She was tried at the Old Bailey, convicted of murder, and on 13 July 1955 was hanged at HMP Holloway, three months after the shooting. She was 28 years old.

In 1967, work began on a major rebuilding of the prison. The original star design, which allowed a single warder to oversee multiple wings, was replaced by accommodation grouped around green spaces, with cells arranged along corridors to allow greater privacy. The ambition was therapeutic. It was not, by most accounts, an ambition the building fulfilled. Multiple inspection reports over the following decades identified persistent problems with safety, hygiene, staff training and mental health provision. The last inspection concluded that the size and poor design made it a very difficult establishment to run.

On 25 November 2015, the then Chancellor of the Exchequer George Osborne announced in his Autumn Statement that Holloway would close, be demolished and the land sold for housing. The reasons given were that its design and physical condition did not provide the best environment for the rehabilitation of offenders. Holloway closed in July 2016. The remaining prisoners were transferred to HMP Downview and HMP Bronzefield, both in Surrey. The closure caused significant distress. Women were imprisoned further from their families, support services built up over years were abruptly discontinued, and many prisoners were deeply unsettled, even suicidal in some cases where it felt that support had been withdrawn.

The year of Holloway's closure, 2016, saw 22 women die in custody across the prison estate, 12 of them by their own hand, the highest number of deaths in women's prisons on record. Whether closure was a contributing factor could not be definitively established. What is beyond doubt is that the women moved at short notice to institutions that were not ready for them found themselves without the networks, the staff relationships and the tailored support that had taken years to build.

★ ★ ★

Myra Hindley died in November 2002, but she has never really left us. Her name remains, more than two decades after her death, a shorthand for a particular category of evil: the evil of the willing participant, the evil of the woman who chose a man's cruelty over every instinct she might have had to protect the children in her path. The photograph taken of her shortly after her arrest in 1965 – straw-blonde hair, flat expression, eyes that appear to return nothing – has become one of the most reproduced images in British cultural history.

Myra Hindley was born on 23 July 1942 in Crumpsall, Manchester, and raised in Gorton, then a working-class area of the city. She met Ian Brady in January 1961 at Millwards Merchandising, the wholesale chemical company in Gorton where both were employed. She was 18. He was 23.

Five children and teenagers were taken from the streets of Manchester and the surrounding area between July 1963 and October 1965. The youngest was ten years old.

On 6 May 1966, Myra Hindley was convicted. She would spend 36 years in prison. And she would spend much of them at Holloway.

For 20 years, neither Brady nor Hindley admitted to the murders of Pauline Reade and Keith Bennett. In 1985, Brady finally confessed. The body of Pauline Reade was eventually recovered from Saddleworth Moor in 1987. Keith Bennett has never been found. His body remains on the moor.

Hindley was held initially at HMP Holloway, where a prison warder named Patricia Cairns fell profoundly in love with her. Cairns and Hindley plotted an escape that came considerably closer to succeeding than has generally been acknowledged. Cairns was convicted at the Old Bailey in 1974 and sentenced to six years for her part in the scheme. Hindley was transferred to HMP Durham, where she later encountered and befriended Rose West, who had been transferred there following her 1995 conviction at Winchester Crown Court. The relationship soured. They became, it is reported, sworn enemies.

The mythology that built up around Hindley during her decades of imprisonment is distinctive: the belief, passed among officers like an inheritance, that her eyes would give her away.

Debbie James has seen those eyes. This is what she found.

'I actually met Myra Hindley when I was at Cookham Wood on escort, took a prisoner down there and had to look round while we were there,' she recalled. 'You wouldn't have recognised her in the street. Very agreeable, mild and inoffensive. You wouldn't look twice at her. People used to say, "Oh, when you see her, you'll know, because her eyes are really evil." But they weren't. They were just ordinary eyes. She was nothing like that picture at all.

'She worked in the hospital as a hospital orderly. A trusted job. The ones in for a long sentence tend to be the ones who don't make a fuss about anything. They get the sentence done and get some quality of life. They just want to get their heads down and get on with it. Those tend to be the ones who get allocated the good jobs. All the notorious prisoners tend to have a lot of friends because people like to be associated with them, because of the notoriety. But I wouldn't say they're genuine friends. They tag on because of the fame.'

It was disturbing to say the least, to imagine Myra Hindley attracting groupies, but we have seen the same thing many times with notorious prisoners.

What Debbie described is a consistent pattern across the women's estate. The reality of notorious prisoners, seen at close range, is almost always a disappointment to anyone expecting visible monstrousness. The crimes exist in one register; the person occupies another. Vanessa Frake-Harris, a former Governor and wonderful contributor to our previous books, with a wealth of knowledge about the social architecture of the women's system, noted something important about the longer-term trajectory of even the most notorious inmates.

'Myra Hindley was working on receptions. She had a job and was back in the general population. At some point you have to rejoin people into society and the general population for their benefit. Keeping someone separate costs money and also isn't good long-term for someone's mental state.'

Hindley's campaign for release was championed at various points by significant figures, among them the prison reformer Lord Longford and the novelist Doris Lessing. Hindley converted to Roman Catholicism. She obtained a degree from the Open University. She presented herself, consistently, as a transformed person. But she became, in a specific and politically significant way, the prisoner who could never be freed: not because of what the law said, but because of what the country felt.

On 15 November 2002, Myra Hindley died in West Suffolk Hospital, Bury St Edmunds, of bronchial pneumonia brought on by respiratory failure. She was 60 years old. She had served 36 years in prison. Keith Bennett's body is still on the moor.

Suzy Dymond-White had done bed watches at Cookham Wood while Hindley was held there, though the prisoner she sat with turned out not to be Hindley. It was another woman serving a very long sentence, on a parallel trajectory. What she found there stayed with her.

'She was so institutionalised,' Suzy told us. 'She had nothing to talk about. Her biggest concern was who was going to wash the landing floors while she was in hospital. Because that was where her life was. She was the wing cleaner. She was so worried that her wing wasn't going to be scrubbed to the level it should be while she wasn't there to do it. But that was her world at that point. We all need to have a role and a purpose, and her purpose was to keep the wing clean. And she wasn't there to do it. It was just really striking.' And then, she said, just Suzy and this woman in a side room for 12 hours, 'Do you want to watch a bit of telly now? Please. Yes. Please don't talk about the floors again.'

Simon had worked at Holloway during the period when one high-profile prisoner was held there. He was clear that managing her presented significant challenges.

'She was very difficult to manage,' he said. 'She was demanding, highly aware of her own notoriety and reputation among the general and prison population, and that created real risks around her safety and placement. She could not be located on ordinary location because the risk to her was too high, so she had to be managed separately and carefully.

'As time went on, she began to form relationships with other women. That was not unusual. In prison, relationships are often about closeness, protection and being seen by someone in a place where normal life has been stripped away. They are not always sexual. Sometimes they are about emotional survival.'

Holloway held other notorious inmates. The death of Peter Connelly (known as Baby P) in August 2007 was one of the most devastating child protection failures in British history. He was just 17 months old and had more than 50 injuries. He had been seen by professionals on more than 60 occasions. He was on the child protection register. None of it saved him.

Peter died at the family home in Tottenham, north London, at the hands of his mother, Tracey Connelly, her partner Steven Barker and Barker's brother, Jason Owen.

Tracey Connelly had already pleaded guilty to causing or allowing the death of a child. Sentencing took place at the Old Bailey on 22 May 2009. She received an indeterminate sentence of imprisonment for public protection, with a minimum term of five years. Barker was convicted of the same charge and also of raping a two-year-old girl in a separate trial, receiving a life sentence with a minimum of ten years. Owen was jailed indefinitely with a minimum of three years.

The public response was immediate and furious. The NSPCC's chief executive described the sentences as too lenient. Lord Laming was commissioned to revisit his earlier recommendations following the death of Victoria Climbié, which had occurred in the same borough in 2000. Peter Connelly's death prompted a reckoning with child protection in Britain that lasted years and reshaped policy and practice across the country.

Connelly first became eligible for parole in August 2012. The board made no recommendation to release her. However, in 2013 she was released on licence, the first of what would become a pattern of release and recall. In 2015 she was returned to custody after breaching the terms of her licence by selling indecent photographs of herself online. Parole reviews in 2015, 2017 and 2019 all resulted in refusal. In March 2022 the Parole Board directed her release for the second time and she was released in July 2022, subject to 20 additional licence conditions including electronic tagging, a curfew, restrictions on her movements, monitored internet and phone use, and a requirement to disclose any intimate relationships to her supervising officers. In late summer 2024 she was recalled to prison for a second time after starting a relationship with a man she had met online without disclosing it to officials. A parole hearing held in public in October 2025 heard Connelly tell the board that she had deleted material from her phone to conceal the relationship, and that she had lied because she feared being rejected by the man if he knew who she was.

She told the board she knew deep down that her son had been being abused by Barker, that she had been too consumed by trying to prove the professionals wrong to act on what she knew, and that she had been a bad mother who had put her own needs first and had failed to protect her children. Steven Barker lost a further parole bid in 2024.

Women such as Connelly, who have committed crimes against children, are treated with particular contempt by other prisoners, and are at a high risk of assault. This can result in them being put in some form of segregation for their own protection. As we know from our books about male prisons, a huge degree of ingenuity goes into finding ways to attack child killers and child sex offenders.

The *Sunday Mirror* reported an account in December 2021 from Emma Tustin's former cellmate Elaine Pritchard, who had shared a cell with her for six weeks while Tustin was on remand. Pritchard told the *Sunday Mirror* that inmates had laced Tustin's meals with salt as payback for what she had done to Arthur, who had himself been poisoned with around 34g of salt before the fatal assault. Pritchard told the newspaper that 'Some of the things we did were cruel – but she was crueller to Arthur so she deserved it.'

Simon also noted the practical risks in managing prisoners whose offences or public profile made them vulnerable. 'When someone is held separately for their own safety or due to their index offence, you have to think about every route by which the wider population could still affect them,' he said. 'That includes things most people would never think about. Food, movement, information, routine. You learn very quickly that security is not just locks and doors. It is knowing where the risks might come from and attempting to mitigate them.' In prison the majority of the work is done by prisoners who are employed in areas such as the kitchen, stores and gardens etc. Prisoners choose their food from a menu of choices and it is recorded and sent to the kitchen. It wouldn't be difficult at all for a prisoner to know where another prisoner was located and contaminate or adulterate their food.

Simon recalled another high-profile prisoner at Holloway, renamed inside the prison for her own protection. 'Then there was an extremely prolific child abuser,' he told us. 'She worked in a nursery on the outside and a paedophile network had preyed on her and groomed her to gain access to the children. I don't think she was necessarily that way inclined herself. She was manipulated into it to impress or ingratiate herself into that group of people. She is an example of how people, for complicated reasons, get used by others who are far more calculating than they are. Paedophiles are enormously manipulative. That is their entire operation.'

Simon remembered another woman at the same prison whose circumstances illustrated the fury that motivates some female prisoners. 'There was a woman who found out that a man in the housing block opposite her had been abusing her children, who had been going over there to play,' he said. 'She got a knife, went over, knocked on the door, stabbed him repeatedly, went back to the lift, went home and carried on as if nothing had happened.

'Her response was violent and criminal, and there is no getting away from that. But you could also see the emotional rupture behind it. Understanding what drove someone does not mean excusing what they did. In prison work you have to hold both things in your mind at once.'

'The Angel of Death', nurse Beverley Allitt, was held briefly at Holloway before being transferred to New Hall. Beverley Allitt was born on 4 October 1968 in Corby Glen, a small village in Lincolnshire. Her childhood, by most accounts, was unremarkable on the surface, though those who later examined her history in forensic detail noted an early and sustained pattern of attention-seeking behaviour that would prove significant. She was a frequent visitor to her local hospital and GP surgery, presenting with ailments that often could not be satisfactorily explained. Despite a deeply problematic profile, and despite the chronic understaffing that was by then endemic in the National Health Service, Allitt was taken on in February 1991 on a temporary six-month contract at Grantham and Kesteven Hospital in Lincolnshire, working as a State Enrolled Nurse on Ward Four, the children's ward. The ward was so short-staffed that on some shifts only two trained nurses covered the day and a single nurse was left to manage the ward alone through the night.

What followed took place over 59 days, between February and April 1991. During that period, Allitt attacked 13 children on Ward Four. Four of them died: Liam Taylor, an infant who had been admitted with a chest infection; Timothy Hardwick, an 11-year-old with cerebral palsy; Becky Phillips, a premature baby of just two months; and Claire Peck, a 15-month-old child with asthma. Nine other children survived her attacks, though not without lasting consequence. Paul Crampton, a five-month-old, was injected with insulin on three separate occasions. The methods she used included the administration of large doses of insulin, the injection of air into the bloodstream to cause embolism, suffocation and the deliberate tampering with ventilators and intravenous medication pumps.

The pattern only became visible because it was so extreme. The number of cardiac arrests on the ward was simply too high to be coincidence, a fact recognised first by consultant paediatrician Dr Porter. By 30 April 1991, the police had been called. Superintendent Stuart Clifton visited the hospital on 1 May and within a short time had identified, by cross-referencing duty rosters with the incidents, that Allitt was the only person present for all

13 cases. She was suspended from duty and arrested in November 1991.

Her trial at Nottingham Crown Court began in February 1993. The jury found Allitt guilty on a number of counts in May 1993: four counts of murder, 11 counts of attempted murder, and 11 counts of causing grievous bodily harm. Mr Justice David Latham sentenced her to 13 concurrent terms of life imprisonment and told her, in terms that admitted no ambiguity, that she was a serious danger to others and was unlikely ever to be considered safe enough to be released.

What happened immediately after sentencing was revealing. Within days of arriving in prison, Allitt stopped eating and drinking entirely. She was transferred to Rampton Secure Hospital in Nottinghamshire, the high-security psychiatric facility where she has remained ever since. In December 2007, Mr Justice Stanley Burnton confirmed the original 30-year minimum tariff that the trial judge had recommended in 1993 but which no Home Secretary had ever formally set. That tariff expired in November 2021. In practice it changes very little. Allitt remains detained under the Mental Health Act at Rampton, where she has been since shortly after her 1993 conviction, and while she is in psychiatric detention rather than prison her case is a matter for a mental health tribunal, not the Parole Board. In October 2023 she applied to be transferred to a mainstream prison, a move that would have opened the door to parole proceedings six months later. The tribunal refused her request on 8 December

2023, ruling that she should remain at Rampton, and stipulated that she could not be reassessed for up to three years. That window opens in late 2026.

Bev Butler was at New Hall when Allitt first arrived. For her, this was not an abstract name from a newspaper. Allitt had murdered a baby from her village.

'Beverley Allitt, yes. She actually killed somebody from the village where I used to live. She murdered one of the babies at Grantham Hospital. So we had to monitor her. She went on hunger strike, and she was in a cell with the door open and we watched her 24/7 before we could get her to Rampton. Beverley Allitt was segregated from the beginning. From the healthcare unit she would have been torn to shreds. She was at New Hall before she got moved on to Rampton. She was intimidating. Very smarmy, wanting to be liked. She had Munchausen's by proxy, didn't she? Everyone was told, don't accept anything from her, don't take sweets from her, don't take anything she offers, because you just never knew what she was capable of. She wasn't allowed to mix with anybody, she was that dangerous.'

'She was chatty, yes. That's what I mean by smarmy. Always wanting to be liked. That was part of the Munchausen's, probably. And she professed her innocence. She didn't do anything. She hadn't harmed them. She didn't want to kill them . . . We knew from the beginning she was going to Rampton. She was that dangerous. Not a nice situation.'

Cath Thompson, who was also present when Allitt

came in, was similarly unequivocal: 'Beverley Allitt, very manipulative. She didn't express remorse. They think in their minds what they did was acceptable. I was in when she first came in. She was very manipulative when I was there. If you had no work pattern, 23 hours a day behind your door, boredom, going into your own head; 23 hours a day to sit and think.'

Vanessa Frake-Harris, who had worked in the Prison Service for many years, was in reception at the time of Allitt's arrival from court and offered a surprising characterisation.

'Beverley Allitt was one of the quietest, mouse-like people. She didn't look like she would say boo to a goose. She was very subdued: the kind of person you would instantly put onto suicide watch.'

Vanessa described Allitt as the mirror image of Lucy Letby in terms of external presentation: in both cases, the outward appearance bore almost no relationship to what the person was convicted of.

Like Letby, Allitt was a carer in whom parents had placed absolute trust. Like Letby, she used insulin and the injection of air into the bloodstream as weapons. Like Letby, her crimes came to light through a pattern of deaths and collapses that simply could not be explained by coincidence. A retired detective involved in the Allitt investigation later described Letby publicly as a copycat murderer, suggesting it was almost as if she had read the Allitt book. Whether or not that was the case, the parallels are striking and disturbing in equal measure.

Vanessa returned to this question too, something that clearly occupied her thinking. 'I always think that these sorts of serial killers like Shipman, Letby, Allitt, they're all in the caring profession. Which I always think is interesting. Is it like the fireman who sets fires or the policeman who rapes and murders? Has it got something to do with that sort of occupation?'

Simon had arrived at Holloway from Feltham, a very different kind of establishment. His first impressions of the place were of somewhere unlike anywhere he had worked in before.

'The first thing that struck me on that initial visit was the quiet,' he told us. 'Feltham is a massive site, a lot of it open. It was built along Californian lines, so all the corridors, called linkways, are open, just barred. In winter, the rain comes in sideways and it is absolutely freezing. There were prisoners everywhere. Gardeners, storemen, kitchen people, all out in the grounds with staff. I walked into Holloway and into the grounds and there was nothing. No one. We went on to A Block and walked all the way around and did not see a single person. All you could really hear was moaning and groaning and calling, and it was just like an 18th-century workhouse. They had no staff. All the units were on patrol, which means one member of staff and all the prisoners locked away.'

His first encounter with a prisoner there was one he described with some amusement.

'My first prisoner was an old, hollow-faced, sunken-eyed woman, obviously a drug addict, with a roll-up hanging out of her mouth. She was walking back from speaking to a colleague and as I got closer, I could see her eyes bugging slightly. She just collapsed forward, and I jumped and caught her. As her head went into my chest, the roll-up burnt a hole in my shirt. She missed my nipple by about half an inch. That was my first experience of Holloway, a burnt shirt, and I got the immediate thought, this is where I was meant to be.'

He noticed, too, that the physical infrastructure was strikingly different from anything he was used to. 'The other thing that struck me immediately was that all their doors were wooden,' he said. 'At Feltham we had huge reinforced steel cell doors. These were wooden doors with normal handles. If you had put me in one of those I would have kicked my way out in under a minute, literally.' The building itself told you a lot about the pressures staff were working under and the risks they were trying to manage.

Despite its limitations, Holloway under the right leadership became considerably better than what Simon had first encountered. The prison developed safer cells, tested new anti-ligature designs from across the estate, and became known in the wider Prison Service for its approach to self-harm and crisis management.

'We were the first female establishment to have safer cells,' he told us. 'We had an entire spur of them. Anti-ligature, indestructible. We used to stress test everything at Holloway. They would bring new designs to us from the wider estate and we would test them to destruction. This was because of the level of self-harm we were dealing with.

I cut hanging and non-hanging women down all day long, who were mostly using their bedsheets and clothing to tie ligatures. You would go in and find them unresponsive. The day was a never-ending mix of violence and self-harm, incredibly draining and difficult to be immersed in, often with multiple incidents happening simultaneously, which all needed managing.

I remember being on the floor with a woman who had fitted and had swallowed her tongue and who was basically choking. I was just in the process of putting my fingers down her throat to try and clear her airway when another alarm was sounded. I was torn between finishing what I was doing without her clamping down on my fingers and needing to rush off to the next incident. That was a typical Holloway day. Another incident occurred at the weekend when there was minimal staff. An alarm sounded and it became apparent that a healthcare prisoner had set her cell on fire and had tied a non-suspended ligature. I attended as one of the few staff on duty and entered the unit to find it filled with smoke. I observed the prisoner on the floor of her cell unresponsive. I entered the cell to establish what was required and was joined by one of the nurses. Between us we performed CPR and managed to resuscitate her and bring her back. As a result of my actions, I was awarded an area managers commendation and my family were invited into the jail, where it was presented to me at a full staff meeting. Cringe!'

He spoke about two governors who shaped what Holloway became in its later years. Tony Hassell had transformed the prison from a place that was by his own description terrible to a level four high-performing establishment. 'He was excellent at bringing in third-sector people and organisations to provide services,' Simon said. 'He was a huge advocate for women, a huge advocate for safer custody and good practice.'

Sue Saunders, a later governor, had left a different kind of mark. 'She was one of the best governors I worked with,' he said. 'One of the most compassionate and lovely people. She was the one who taught me about punishment in terms of approach. Her view was: we are not going to punish people if they can show that they have understood why they ended up in this situation. If they can demonstrate contrition and genuine understanding, we will treat it as learning rather than punishment. She would have discussions with me beforehand, off the record, about particular individuals, both staff and prisoners and how things had manifested, and we would together decide what the most appropriate course of action would be. The learning and contrition aspects were always at the forefront of how we dealt with things and it was progressive and successful.'

The self-harm Simon managed daily had its most devastating failures as well as its near-misses. Another prisoner was a small Irish woman, a drug addict who was beginning to find her way when she died.

'She killed herself and it was just awful and horrible because it was such a waste,' he told us. 'She was a lovely woman. After we cut her down I spent the day with her body, to make sure that everything was done properly and that she was respected as a person, even in death. That was really important to me.'

The point in a recovery arc when someone is most at risk, he said, 'was not the bottom of the curve. It was when they started making progress. That was when they were at the highest risk of killing themselves. She had killed herself at exactly that moment. Another example of something which left a deep mark on me and how I approached my job.'

He described one incident in the segregation unit that illustrated both the speed at which violence could arrive and the vulnerability of healthcare staff who believed a familiar relationship would hold under any conditions.

He had accompanied a nurse to give medication to a volatile prisoner in the segregation area. He had advised giving the medication through the hatch rather than entering the cell. The nurse declined, saying the prisoner knew her. We asked what happened. 'As soon as I had opened the door, this woman sprang – literally sprang towards the nurse, her feet left the ground – and the nurse was there, and I just had to react. And I got both fists in my face,' he told us. 'We both fell, and I fell on top of her, and we both slid across the floor, and I ended up smashing my face into the radiator at the back of the cell. They were finned radiators. It was another example of how a situation can flip and become so deadly. I still have a scar across my nose from that individual and she was never prosecuted for the assault. It was reported to the police, but when they came to take her out of the jail to interview her with a view to charging her she was sat on the floor of her cell eating a bowl of her own excrement and vomit. They took one look and said "no way" and just like that they deemed it NFA or "no further action". It was not in the public interest as she was clearly disturbed and the likelihood of her being able to participate in the process was limited.'

He recalled a hostage situation at Holloway that he resolved by departing entirely from the approved protocol, in a way that only worked because of the specific authority he had built over years in the prison. 'I came slightly later to the party, and I quickly worked out who the two perpetrators were, and I knew it was not as serious a situation as it presented itself as. There were staff kitted up on both sides of the cell door in full riot gear. I took one look and just opened the door, walked into the cell, and said: "you, come now; you, come now; we are going to the seg." And that was it. It is against every protocol in the book, but when you know your onions and you know what you are dealing with, you can be confident your actions are going to end the right way. I was told off very badly for it afterwards but the end result justified my actions. This would become my mantra and when it came to judgement calls and my own perception of the resolution I would tend to ask for forgiveness after the fact rather than permission beforehand.'

Women do not try to escape from closed prisons often. The E-list – the escape list – carries consequences so severe that most prisoners regard it as a deterrent. Simon explained what being placed on that list meant in practice.

'When you are on the E-list, you have to wear the yellow and green bumblebee suit, as we called it,' he said. 'The prisoner is then referred to by staff and on the radio as "Book One". Whenever you move anywhere you need an officer and that officer needs permission to move Book One. That individual is not allowed anything in their cell overnight whatsoever. The cell has to be completely stripped. One change of soft clothes. All the cutlery and everything has to be out of the cell at night. Staff have to check and double-check, check all the walls, check all the fixtures and fittings. I used to do LBBs – locks, bolts and bars – every day, go and check the fabric of the cell, check the equipment, make sure everything works. Having that awareness of what is going on is one of the most valuable things. Knowledge is currency, knowledge is power, always.'

And yet it happened. During Simon's time at Holloway, several women tried, and one came considerably closer than she should have.

'A woman we believed had escaped actually concealed herself within the education department,' he told us. 'Initially the belief was that she had disguised herself as a member of the public and managed to get through the staff airlock and conceal herself within a larger group of people going out. There was another added dimension: an off-the-record rumour or gossip that this was all set up by one of the teachers, who potentially was having a relationship with this particular prisoner, and they would find her in his flat. So the police raided his flat and she wasn't there.

'Anyway, very long story short. She had managed to conceal herself within the education department by moving one of the lockers just very slightly. It created a very small pocket of space behind it, but visually it looked flush against the wall. She had taken food left by staff from different drawers and they found bags of waste because the toilet doors were locked. She survived there for a good few days until the dogs sniffed her out. We went in and stripped each room until we found her.

'We had another prisoner who managed to get over the wall by the chapel as it wasn't as high or as well-protected as the other walls. She jumped down and broke both her ankles. A member of the public found her, a woman screaming outside the prison. And on a different occasion there was another prisoner who attempted to escape while on an external hospital escort. She asked the staff to go to the toilet and then she jumped out of a window and also damaged herself quite badly.'

We found these stories incredibly unsettling. 'Women are not as prolific in that regard,' Simon noted. 'It is a very rare thing because the consequences of escape are huge.'

* * *

Holloway's history contains layers that most of those who worked there never discovered. Simon had been there a good while before he came across one of them. 'There was a weird, unused, blocked-off upper-floor area with a spiral staircase that used to house female IRA prisoners years ago. It had all been decommissioned and was located where the current mother and baby unit was. You went up a weird spiral staircase and there was a whole unit up there. Very odd, very creepy. The mother and baby unit was the exercise yard for the IRA prisoners and it was completely outside, hemmed in, metal-barred ceiling and walls. I had been there a good while before I discovered it.'

Cath, who had joined the service in 1985 and been posted to Holloway as one of her first assignments, arrived during the period when women connected to the IRA were held there. She had been on 12 months' probation when they were present, which meant she was not part of the detail that guarded them, but she knew the staff who were. The subject, she told us, was not one those officers discussed readily, then or later.

Among the prisoners Simon encountered at Holloway were several whose circumstances captured something particular about how the women's estate works. Vicky Pryce, the economist and former wife of Cabinet minister Chris Huhne, had been convicted of perverting the course of justice in 2013 and arrived in Holloway to considerable attention from the media and the prisoner population.

'Vicky Pryce – when she arrived they were like bees round honey, of course,' he said. 'Because this woman is not a criminal. She's a very literate, very learned, very clever woman. And she's not like them at all in any way. And she was a target, definitely. But give her her dues – she settled very nicely. And she had her own little group. And to be fair, she got stuck on the lifers' unit, where they're all slightly older, a bit more system-aware, but more settled.'

Then there was the young woman he had managed on the lifers' unit, described to us as Britain's youngest double murderer at the time. 'She was a young offender, a tiny girl, who murdered her father and his girlfriend. She stabbed them to death. She caused me a lot of trouble because she was very young, had a life sentence, and was just reckless. Very reckless. People only really regret what they have done when the door shuts behind them. With some it takes years, with some it never really comes.' He's talking about Lorraine Thorpe, who had formed a friendship with our contributor, Anastasia Severn.

Simon has followed her case at a distance in the years since. 'She's been re-categorised and she's going to open conditions,' he said. 'She's probably 30 now, something like that. I dealt with her when she was 17, 18. She was a kid, and her father conducted himself in not a nice way. She didn't have the capacity to express what she felt in any other way than to kill him, and his girlfriend as well. She had no tenderness. She just had horrible shit. And that manifested itself in her killing her father and his girlfriend. And then going through being a kid, a teenager, who had ruined their life and had to be in this shitty place every single day. She tried to kill herself so many times. I totally get it. She wasn't supported by anyone really. She hadn't even lived her life – the life she'd lived had been horrible, abusive, and a struggle. Just pure survival.'

Cath arrived at Holloway in 1985, having trained for a month and spent time at Manchester first. She was 22 years old, and her account of those early years at the prison captures something of what it meant to be thrown into the women's estate young and largely unprepared.

She hated London, she told us, and found the women temperamental in ways she had not encountered in training. It came out, she said, in cut-ups, in fights, in aggression. 'You never knew what you were unlocking,' she told us. 'Training did not prepare me at all. They do try and blag you. An officer advised me, don't say it's your first posting. You get the occasional threat. I used to stutter and go bright red. I had an officer I could go to if I had any problem. You were on 12 months' probation from the day you joined. We always backed each other up.'

On the question of age, she was characteristically direct. 'I think age needs putting up,' she told us. 'Just turned 22 in 1985 is too young. You're telling older women what to do – I put on bravado; my knees were knocking. Should be at least 25. Everything is totally arse back to front.'

Among the cases that stayed with her from those years was a woman she had escorted to court. 'She was the one who set fire to women's toilets – set fire to the toilets at railway stations,' Cath told us. 'Arson with intent. She got sectioned in the end, sent to Rampton.' But while she was at Holloway, Cath told us, she had whispered to her when they were in the dock: 'What is it with female toilets, do you not like them?' 'And she laughed,' Cath said. The woman's behaviour was, she thought, rooted in a mental state rather than a decision. 'Them that can't help what they're doing – I could work with them all day.'

Dainya Ebanks was placed on the Young Offender wing at Holloway, A3. We have kept what she shared with us in her own, very powerful, words:

My experience in HMP Holloway, on the YOI wing (A3), was nothing like I expected. If I had to describe it honestly, it felt like a mix between a circus and a children's home – loud, chaotic, unpredictable. But underneath all that noise, there was something heavier: pain, confusion and instability that never really switched off.

It wasn't what people on the outside picture when they think of prison. These weren't just hardened criminals. These were young women, aged between 18 and 21, still figuring themselves out, still carrying things they hadn't processed. Some were dealing with drug addiction, others with alcohol dependency. Some were foreign nationals caught up in drug smuggling. Others had been involved in knife crime. And then there were girls who had simply made a few bad decisions and ended up there. There was no one type of person. That's what stood out the most.

I was placed in a dorm rather than a single cell. Five beds in one room, with just one toilet. No privacy, no escape, no real sense of control. You don't get to choose who you live with, and you don't know who's coming next. Every new person brings a different energy, different habits, different attitudes – and in a space that small, that matters.

In terms of violence, I didn't experience much directly on A3. It was more arguments than anything else – over relationships, over borrowed clothes, over small misunderstandings that escalated quickly. When you're confined, emotions don't have space to breathe. But what affected me more than the arguments was the emotional distress. Seeing women self-harm. Walking around with visible scars on their arms. Some fresh, some old. Hearing someone screaming behind a door, crying, or threatening to hurt themselves. Seeing someone barricade themselves in, completely overwhelmed. At that point in my life, that was new to me. It stays with you.

One of the hardest things to witness was visits. Watching the mums spend time with their children – holding them, playing with them, trying to be present in that small window of time – and then having to say goodbye. You'd see them holding it together during the visit, putting on a brave face. But when they came back on to the wing, that's when it hit them. The crying, the silence, the emptiness after.

After a while, I realised I needed space. So I requested a single cell. Because I was on enhanced status – a red band – I had a bit more privilege, and eventually I was able to move. That change made a real difference. Having my own space gave me back a sense of control. A place where I could think, reset, and just be still without constantly managing other people's energy.

Looking back, Holloway wasn't just about serving time. It was an environment that exposed me to so many *different realities – different people, different struggles, different coping mechanisms. It forced me to observe, to adapt, and to understand people on a deeper level. It taught me the importance of boundaries. The value of good relationships. How much your environment can shape your mindset if you let it. But it also showed me something else. Even in a place like that, there can still be moments of care. Moments of connection. Moments of growth.*

Neah Tuohy arrived at Holloway on remand, cycling back and forth to court at Snaresbrook while the evidence against her was being tested. She had prepared herself, she thought, for what was coming.

Her earliest encounters with the system had begun long before Holloway. The first thing had been graffiti, she said. 'Yeah, so it was around my postcode, all over about – stupid, really, 'cause my mum, three grand fine, absolutely furious, she was. All on camera. I don't know. I just think – it's not happening.' She had got arrested for criminal damage, she said. 'The charge was on graffiti, it was criminal damage, 'cause it was on a bus. And the postcode everywhere. You just think, some of this wouldn't happen now. There's no way that they'd have any sort of, you know, that level of kind of punishment for something like that.'

Her family background had given her the kind of preparation for physical confrontation that served her in custody even as it had contributed to landing her there. 'My mum just took it around, good – love her, close to her. We are quite close now, yeah, but we never used to be. At all. So it was pretty much on my own, kind of grown up. I've got older brothers and stuff, but I was a lot younger than them. Just girls. You know, just quite different. There was, like, teenage boys who don't want to, kind of, raise their little sister knocking around.' So she was the youngest?, we asked. 'I'm the youngest, a load of brothers, yeah. So they always taught me to fight. Stick up for myself. The guy puts their hands on you, you hit them back. You know, things like that. They thought they was doing really well. Really, you know, big brother stuff. And then I'd end up in prison and say, you know, bloody hell. I'd say, but you – I know. And they'd go, no, like, this is – my brother, even if you saw everyone they'd talk to, he'd go massively responsible for a lot of decisions I've made in my life.' She told him to forget it now, she said. 'But he does, because he did always teach me that. But it's not all down to him, anyway. There are only people just trying to do the best with what they've got. Sometimes people don't have the best start themselves, do they? Like my mum and my dad and stuff. I don't hold too much against them for the life that I had. I used to. A lot. Now I realise they just do what they can with what they've got.

I was on remand for about ten months before I was found guilty, eight of them at Holloway,' she told us. 'The way the trial was going, and what I could see going in and out of evidence and how things were being presented, I kind of knew by that point how it was going and that I was going to end up with a guilty verdict and it was going to be a long time. But even when they said it, I still couldn't believe what they'd found me guilty of. I had medical evidence proving he never got injured when he was on the floor. They were saying it was intent, which means he got injured on the floor from a fall. The medical evidence supported one slice, not a wound consistent with being on the floor. So whatever they thought about me, I thought the truth is the truth and they can't get around that. I had never really seen how people get convicted of things that obviously haven't happened.'

What she took from the years that followed, she told us, was a reckoning with who she had become in custody versus who she wanted to be. 'You get to a point where it's like, why would you feed what grows? Which is tough. 'Cause first of all, I was battling between who I wanted to be, needed to be, and who I had to be to survive. So that made me worry about, you know, getting out. But then luckily, the last two years was Covid, so I managed to be on my own the whole time – tore me apart, but then I didn't have the worry. I could go fully into one, you know, really working on myself.'

She reflected on something she had wanted to do with all of it once she was ready. 'I don't really talk about it any more. I'd like to do a book one day. And then I thought – I also thought that when I'm ready, I'll go into it. I mean, I talk about, like, ADHD in general, but I don't – I don't talk about the stuff that we're talking about. You've got to go there though. You've got to really go there to talk about it.'

Officers had to develop personae for survival just as

much as prisoners in Neah's view. 'Because if you're a bit timid, or whatever, as an officer – if you look like someone who's going to be taken advantage of, as a prisoner or as staff, you're going to get manipulated, unfortunately.' It was the same thing, she said, that happened to prisoners coming out. 'If you survive in there by being, very violent, kind of scary, or whatever, then obviously that, as you say, then, is that really becoming who you are when you come out? Because you can't be like that for how many hours a day, and you'd be pretending all the time, it's gonna become an actual part of your character.' She was thoughtful for a moment. She told us she had a history of violence, and she had had a violent edge in her, and that was what she had needed to get rid of. 'Walking away, why I was like that. Not being more – I think I'm not more of it every day, but the loudest person in the room is often the weakest. But then at the same time, in prison, you can't really be the quiet one either.'

She described a period after release when she could not cope, having very negative thoughts and what she eventually did about it. She was in a really bad moment. 'I kept going down the police station, begging them to take me off the street and put me back in. And then I remember when they did, and I'd finally got put back in. And finally – me, I'll finally want it, 'cause I was on tag, and I made sure I didn't go home for ten days. Just waiting and waiting for the warrant to come through. And on the tenth day when it finally did, and when that door shut, I never felt peace like it in my whole life. Yeah.

I'd never felt safe. I'd never felt safe like that in my whole life. Knowing that not only that I couldn't get into any situation, but no one could also hurt me, and I don't know, it's just – it's really powerful. That's such a weird feeling. Yeah. Really, really sad.'

When the foreman of the jury came back in and said guilty, she told us, she did agree. She had known, she said, by that point how it was heading. 'But even when they did say it,' she said, 'I still couldn't believe it for what they'd found me guilty of.'

After she had been sentenced and left Holloway, she heard later about what happened on the wing. There was a moment of silence when the officers brought out the *Sun* with her verdict in it. All the girls found out. One of the officers – it was like a pin-drop moment, everyone went quiet. It was really sad. Girls she had stayed in contact with wrote to her from other prisons and told her about it afterwards. 'That was something,' she said.

Interestingly, she found Holloway weirdly domestic. 'Out of all the prisons, Holloway was the most like home,' she told us. 'Which is so odd, because it was London and it just had this sense of community about it. But the conditions were terrible. That was why it got shut down. I used to hand-wash my own towels because people would steal them. There were faeces in the bathrooms and showers. Really dirty, nasty place. But on the other hand you'd rather be there than anywhere else. There was a constant sense of safety there, which is strange given everything. The turnaround was so quick. There were a lot of drugs in there. You'd go off the landing and come back to someone new in your cell.'

She described the physical conditions inside with precision. The windows cracked with condensation. If you were on the top bunk, in winter it would be dripping from the ceiling. But somehow, she said, you felt safer there than you expected to. She thought Holloway had had some quite good governors over the years and had been normally quite well-run in terms of the direction from the top. 'And that's why everyone, I think, was quite sad when they were shutting it down.'

The moment when Holloway's closure was announced in 2016 is something Simon described as among the most traumatic of his working life.

'When Holloway closed, it was the best-kept secret in the world,' he said. 'Even the unions did not know. We all got called into the boardroom. All the heads of functions were there. In walked the area manager, Nick Pascoe, and this very short, impish, black-suited woman – that was Emily Thomas, the Governor of Isis. Nick Pascoe addressed the room and said: "While we are here, the Secretary of State is in Parliament making a statement. They are going to close Holloway." The woman opposite me, the head of probation, burst into tears. Nobody could believe it. When I think back on that moment, that was when my life as it had been ended. It was one of the most traumatic things I have experienced. Being in that room was just pure trauma. And even now I still do not understand how they managed to keep that particular closure secret from everyone. The ones I felt most sorry for were the women – they relied on the prison, on the staff, on the fact that this was a place of sanctuary, of refuge, and now that was being taken away.'

The women displaced by Holloway's closure were moved to prisons that were not ready for them, to places further from their families, their support networks and the city they knew. HMP Peterborough, purpose-built and privately managed, received a significant number of them.

CHAPTER 4

HMP Peterborough

'At Peterborough I had Jadine with me, but back in my cell I also had Junior, who I had been pregnant with when the incident happened and had delivered while I was at Styal. So I had two babies in a cell. Jadine is screaming. Junior is restless. There is no space, there is nothing. I do not know how I did it, honestly. I do not.'
YVONNE SIMPSON

HMP Peterborough is a Category B private prison for men, and a closed prison for women and female young offenders, located in Peterborough, Cambridgeshire. Operated by Sodexo Justice Services, it is the only dual purpose-built prison in the United Kingdom designed to hold both males and females, though the two populations have no contact with one another. It opened in 2005 with capacity for 360 women and 480 men, and has a mother and baby unit on site, staffed by both operational and non-operational teams reporting to the MBU and Perinatal Service Manager.

The prison stands on the former site of the Baker Perkins

engineering works, the Westwood Works, which relocated from London to Peterborough in 1904 and spent the better part of the 20th century as one of the city's largest employers, manufacturing food processing machinery for bakery and confectionery industries worldwide. The works employed thousands at their height. By the late 1980s, the company had been absorbed into APV and relocated to new premises, leaving the Westwood site to be cleared. HMP Peterborough opened on the brownfield site on 28 March 2005, under a 25-year contract awarded by the Ministry of Justice and operated by Sodexo Justice Services. Its opening was met with resistance from local residents, but it has become an important local employer and a success story. It proceeded regardless and became what it remains: the only prison in the United Kingdom purpose-built to hold men and women on the same site, their populations kept in strict separation at all times.

In the decades since its opening, the women's side of Peterborough has held prisoners whose cases drew sustained national attention. Among the earliest was Chelsea O'Mahoney, convicted in 2005 as part of the group responsible for the manslaughter of David Morley on the South Bank. Emma Tustin was convicted in 2021 of the murder of six-year-old Arthur Labinjo-Hughes, her partner's son, whose death after prolonged abuse prompted renewed calls for reform of child protection processes. She received a life sentence with a minimum of 29 years. Fiona Beal, a primary school teacher, who murdered her partner, Nicholas Billingham, in 2021, buried his body in the back garden of their home in Northampton, and maintained for months that he had simply left her.

The male and female prisons are mirror images of one another, two institutions sharing a perimeter wall but nothing else. The prison is tucked away behind an industrial estate, more discreetly located than many others on the estate. From the outside, little signals what is inside, but in many ways, it serves as a model of what can be achieved in a modern, purpose-built women's prison.

Within the women's side, the education department is the size of a school. The emphasis throughout is on learning and participation. Artwork by the women is all over the prison. There is a very well-stocked library. On the landings, posters display details of the open prisons that are so desirable in comparison – Eastwood Park and Askham Grange – visible to every woman who passes. Each wing has two storeys of cells. The cells are all the same: a basic bed with a blue mattress, a toilet without a lid, a sink, a mirror, some storage for clothing, a desk and a chair, and an intercom. A double room has the same, with a bunk on top of the other bed and a shared toilet. There is a segregation area on what staff call Main Street, alongside education, healthcare and the gym. Outside the landings, there are gardens, which the women keep.

Security is very tight. Everyone goes through the same procedure from the director down. The technology for prisoners is impressive, too, including the portal, a standing unit that allows electronic access to the canteen, work, medical records, the chaplain, visits – everything.

Some women's cells are filthy. Others are pristine, like show homes. The distance between them is the distance between two entirely different experiences of the same building.

Former inmates consistently describe a buzz in the morning, a basic breakfast, maybe the gym. It gets very busy around 8.30 as women make their way to their jobs. Release on temporary licence operates at Peterborough: some women can go out to work. Association runs until around 7pm. There is a pool table.

Nestled near the entrance with a sloping roof is the mother and baby unit where our contributor Yvonne Simpson had such memorable experiences. The unit has its own kitchen, dining room and playroom. Cells within it have an ensuite with a door. The doors are not locked. Every cell has an intercom.

As Yvonne explained, the mother and baby unit is rarely full, because it is hard to get in. Any application has to go to a board. It is also easy to lose a place there. The stakes could not be higher, and the margin for error is that thin.

Yvonne had two babies in that unit.

'I have a hair salon,' she told us, 'and I was running it with my mum. So when I came back, I was carrying on doing that. Psychology had always interested me anyway. And because of my experience, and there's a lot I'd heard from women in there, I just thought, I need to do more. So I started with the Open University. I left school without any qualifications. I started off doing that part-time, then

I went to Wolverhampton.' Her dream, she said, was to open a secure unit for women where they could be convicted or sentenced with their children. She had been to various funding bodies about it. 'Unfortunately, it fell through. It was really sad. So now I just offer my free time. It's not even paid time. I'm doing it pro bono.'

Her life, she told us, was complicated. She had six children. She had spent ten years with a partner who had been emotionally abusive; when the relationship ended and she met someone new, he had taken their daughter away. She had been running the hair salon, managing everything, and the custody situation had been an open wound throughout.

Her first night at Styal was in December, seven months pregnant. All she wanted was a phone call to her children. Getting that call took more effort than it should have. 'I went down to the first night centre and I said, it is nearly Christmas. Can I please make a call? In the end I said, have you got children? Please let me speak to my kids. After a lot of back and forth, an officer came round after about two minutes. She never sat with me. That was Styal. It should just have been a given anyway. Just a two-minute phone call. Where is the humanity?'

The strip search on arrival she described without softening. 'The strip search when you come in is designed to humiliate. It keeps you down from the minute you arrive. And you are pregnant on top of that. You are bending over, everything. I know women are used to certain things through childbirth and that, but this is on completely different terms. And yeah, it does feel designed to degrade you from the start.'

At Peterborough, among the women she encountered was one whose case she returned to more than once. 'I met a woman,' she told us. 'She had killed her sons. She was quite timid. She was in there for the final part of her sentence – she came out just after me, actually. But she had so much evidence – people saw the doctors and things.' She reflected on it. 'She just snapped. How absolutely horrible. It's not as if she'd be a danger to anyone else.'

She spoke about what she remembered of the communal dining arrangements at Styal before her move to Peterborough. 'At Styal, the food is brought in. The whole house sits together in the dining room. And then you have your living room. I remember it. You walked in, it was like a little porch below, and then it was like one side of it and then another side of it. And there were just living rooms and settees over.'

On the management of the different prisons, she made an observation about who ran them. 'It's Serco at Styal. With the other two – G4S, but it's private. The other two were private as well, no?' It had been weird, she said, going back to the old-time staff compared to what she'd found at Styal: 'That was a contrast at Styal. They were very good.'

Of the business she had been trying to keep going through all of this, she was honest about the reality. 'Honey, it was just on a hat and a prayer. It's just surreal. Absolutely surreal. So in a way I was lucky; in a way I don't have time to freeze. For me, I asked to do it really.'

On access to the chaplain in those early days at Peterborough, Yvonne said it had been the one thing that had helped her manage the immediate shock. 'Yeah. The imam or the priest.' She had talked to the chaplain when she first arrived, she told us. 'Because I was so stressed about the kids. And I think someone needed something. I survived, as well. That's good. So I did have that support. Yeah.'

And on the simple logistical difficulty of family getting to her – a point that applied equally to Styal, to Peterborough, to all of it: 'It's not like you're booking into the nearest Premier Inn. I mean, you just go where you're sent. I can't get there. I know, I understand. It's always hard and weird getting into these places anyway. Always. Especially if you don't drive. My mum didn't drive. But it's just, when you get there, it's a nightmare.'

Yvonne was moved from HMP Styal to HMP Peterborough after giving birth to her daughter Jadine while in custody. She described the conditions on the mother and baby unit in the quietly devastating manner that her soft Black Country accent and lived experience grant her.

'There was no room at Styal's mother and baby unit, so I was moved to Peterborough,' she told us. 'The mother and baby unit there was just one corridor. Two windows in the whole place and just a smell. You had your cell, a bathroom, a small kitchen area and that corridor. That was it. There were no toys, nothing for the baby. You make your own entertainment. I was never locked in the room but I never left that corridor either. You would not have believed it.'

The oversight that came with being in a mother and baby unit was something she found difficult in a particular way. 'When you are in the mother and baby unit, you are watched all the time. Are you feeding? When did you last feed? Is the baby gaining weight? It is monitored. Some women in that position genuinely cannot cope, and I understand why that monitoring exists. But for me, going from running my own business, managing everything, to having my every movement scrutinised, that was one of the hardest things to adjust to.'

The full picture of her situation was starker still, not just because of the challenges of the environment but because of the challenges of two very young children. 'At Peterborough I had Jadine with me, but I also had Junior. So I had two babies in a cell. Jadine is screaming. Junior is restless. There is no space, there is nothing. I do not know how I did it, honestly. I do not.'

She described the postnatal depression that followed, and the calculation she made about how to manage it. 'I had postnatal depression. I did not let it show because I was being watched and I did not want them to take Jadine. So I just held it together as best I could. Even when I had Junior, I cried every day. Every single day. I believe that the trauma I went through during that pregnancy affected him. When babies are born to mothers going through severe trauma, it can affect the child's development and

DNA. Junior had difficulties that I trace back to that.' She eventually moved through Peterborough to Askham Grange open prison, where she served the final part of her sentence.

The consequences of her imprisonment extended across the whole of her family. 'I am passionate about the children. They are the unseen victims. I had three older children who were hurt that I only saw the younger ones. I lost custody of my older children.

Peterborough is defined by what it is: a dual-sex institution, modern and efficiently run. It has seen notable improvements in pastoral care and education facilities even since Yvonne's time, and other contributors who had passed through it were largely positive when describing it to us. South of London, meanwhile, is a prison built solely for women. The largest in Europe: HMP Bronzefield.

CHAPTER 5

HMP Bronzefield

*'She's not how you'd imagine. She's got a little
Mohican, like a skinhead, absolute machine in the
gym. Really, really petite. But rock solid.'*
NEAH TUOHY

Private management was Bronzefield's founding con-dition, and it has shaped the place in ways that those who have lived and worked there described to us with a consistency that is hard to ignore.

HMP Bronzefield is an adult and young offender female prison located on the outskirts of Ashford, not far from Heathrow Airport. Bronzefield is officially in Surrey, despite the close Middlesex link. It is the only purpose-built private prison solely for women in the United Kingdom, the largest female prison in Europe, and is operated by Sodexo Justice Services. It holds up to 572 women, divided across four house blocks of around 130 each, with 17 beds in healthcare, a care and separation unit, and a mother and baby unit accommodating 12 women and 13 babies (up to 18 months old). Its annual report for 2017/18 showed a cost per prisoner of £66,294, at least £10,000 higher than any other women's prison in England and Wales. Multiple deaths in custody have raised serious concerns about healthcare provision and duty of care.

The site was originally occupied by the West London District School, a residential institution for orphaned children established in 1872. In 1961 it was transformed into Ashford Remand Centre, a detention facility for boys. HMP Bronzefield opened on the cleared site in June 2004, the first prison in the United Kingdom designed and built from the ground up solely for women. A 77-bed unit was added in 2009, bringing capacity to over 500. It is one of only three establishments in the female estate approved to hold restricted status prisoners, the others being HMP Low Newton in County Durham and HMP New Hall in West Yorkshire.

Since its opening, Bronzefield has held some of the most closely scrutinised women in the British penal system. Roshonara Choudhry, sentenced to life imprisonment in 2010 for the attempted murder of Labour MP Stephen Timms – stabbed at his constituency surgery after Choudhry had radicalised herself online without contact with any external organisation – was sent there as a restricted status prisoner. Tracey Connelly served part of her sentence at the prison before transfer to HMP Low Newton. Karen Matthews, who staged the abduction of her own daughter Shannon in 2008 in pursuit of a £50,000 reward, was held there. Lucy Letby, convicted in August 2023 of murdering seven infants on the neonatal unit at the Countess of Chester Hospital, was transferred to Bronzefield from HMP New Hall. And it is Bronzefield that has held, since her sentencing in February 2014, Joanna Dennehy.

Simon, who had managed the push to establish a restricted status unit at Holloway before it was reallocated to Bronzefield, described what the unit means in practice. 'Women aren't categorised in the same way as men,' he told us. 'And in Bronzefield, they have what's called a Restricted Status Unit. Which means that these women are effectively Cat A prisoners. Their escape would be catastrophic in the same way that a Cat A escape would be catastrophic. They live in a unit in HMP Bronzefield – much more secure, the processes are much more rigorous, the searching is more rigorous, and the conditions they live in are much more scrutinised. They are under a lot more monitoring and surveillance than your average normal prisoner. We were going to have a restricted status unit at Holloway, and they decided it wasn't going to be Holloway, it was going to be Bronzefield. So we dodged that bullet because we were the dumping ground for the problems of all the other female jails. We took them from everywhere and if a woman was deemed "unmanageable" across the estate she would undoubtedly end up on a van to Holloway. We took them from other segregation units and also healthcare centres. Very damaged and unwell women but we worked with them all and tried our best for them to progress, which many of them did. I believe the unit at Bronzefield is the only one across the women's estate – a bit like the unit within a unit at HMP Belmarsh, a bespoke element for super high risk.'

Joanna Christine Dennehy was born in August 1982 in St Albans, Hertfordshire. She grew up in Harpenden, in circumstances that offered no obvious clue to what she would become. She left home at 15, and the downward trajectory that followed was steep and unrelenting. She became involved with an older man, John Treanor, with whom she had two children. The relationship became violent. By her mid-twenties she was heavily involved in alcohol and drugs, and had accumulated criminal convictions for assault and for owning a dangerous dog. She had been placed under the supervision of the Probation Service. It was on probation, in March 2013, that she began to kill.

The murders were carried out over ten days in March and early April of that year, in and around Peterborough. The killings became known in the press as the Peterborough Ditch Murders. The first to die was Lukasz Slaboszewski, a 31-year-old Polish national who had met Dennehy in Peterborough through a shared interest in alcohol and drugs, and who had been led to believe she was his new girlfriend. She invited him to a house and blindfolded him, telling him it was a game. Then she stabbed him in the heart. His body was stored in a wheelie bin while she moved on to her next victim. John Chapman was 56 years old, a housemate of Dennehy's who had served in the Falklands War. He was murdered on 29 March 2013. Later that same day, Dennehy killed Kevin Lee, her 48-year-old landlord and lover, a property developer with a wife and family who had been unaware of his relationship with her. She dumped Lee's body near Newborough, but not before dressing it in a black sequined dress, an act of deliberate post-mortem humiliation. The bodies of Slaboszewski and Chapman were discovered a few days later in a drainage ditch near Thorney. Forensic analysis confirmed the same knife had been used in all three killings.

Dennehy did not stop. Accompanied by her accomplice Gary Richards, she drove to Hereford, where over the course of a single afternoon she stabbed two complete strangers, Robin Bereza and John Rogers, both of whom had been walking their dogs. Both survived. She was arrested on 2 April 2013. She is reported to have laughed and joked with the police officer who processed her during booking. Later she told investigators that she had intended to kill nine people in total.

Prison staff discovered a detailed escape plot in Dennehy's diary during her time on remand. The plan involved murdering a female prison officer, severing one of the officer's fingers and using the amputated digit to fool the biometric security system. The plan was not a fantasy. It was operational, specific and chilling. As a result of its discovery, Dennehy was placed in solitary confinement from September 2013 and remained there through and beyond the conclusion of her court proceedings until September 2015, a period of approximately two years.

On 18 November 2013, Joanna Dennehy pleaded

guilty to all charges: three counts of murder and two counts of attempted murder. She went straight to the Old Bailey for sentencing. During the proceedings she was observed to laugh. She stood at one point and declared that she did not want to be controlled by anybody. On 28 February 2014, Mr Justice Spencer passed sentence. He described her as a cruel, calculating, selfish and manipulative serial killer. He noted that she had been diagnosed with paraphilic sadomasochism, a disorder characterised by the derivation of sexual pleasure from the infliction of pain and humiliation on others. He noted also that her crimes had been planned and premeditated, that she had shown absolutely no remorse, and that she had stated openly that she had enjoyed killing. He sentenced her to life imprisonment with a whole-life order. She became only the third woman in British legal history to receive such a sentence, following Myra Hindley and Rosemary West. Lucy Letby has since become the fourth.

Since her incarceration, Dennehy's behaviour in prison has continued to reflect the personality disorders with which she was diagnosed before sentencing. In 2018, she requested permission to marry a fellow prisoner, Hayley Palmer, a request that alarmed Palmer's family, who feared for her safety. Later that same year, Dennehy and Palmer reportedly attempted a suicide pact. In 2019, Dennehy was transferred to HMP Low Newton in County Durham. Reports at the time claimed that upon her arrival she had threatened Rosemary West, who was subsequently moved to another institution. The government denied that any such threat had been made or acted upon.

Two of our contributors had followed Dennehy's case long before she arrived at Bronzefield. A third had watched her there directly.

For our previous book, *Inside Wakefield Prison*, we had asked Geoffrey Wansell for his view of Dennehy's situation. Geoffrey is an extraordinarily well-informed and intelligent crime writer, TV presenter and movie producer. He did not mince his words to us about Dennehy.

'Take Joanna Dennehy. She made no secret of the fact she was guilty; she made no secret of the fact that she enjoyed killing them.'

Suzy Dymond-White offered us her perspective on the dynamic Dennehy had created inside, too. 'Joanna Dennehy is a good example of a notorious prisoner coming in and giving women a different kind of status opportunity,' she said. 'If you've got your face in the newspapers and everyone knows your name, that's one way of being at the top of the pecking order in a women's prison. She said herself before she went in that she was obsessed by her publicity, her profile, her notoriety.'

Neah was housed on the same block. She had watched Dennehy at close quarters – in the exercise yard, in the gym, in the changing rooms – and had something she had been wanting to ask her.

'Obviously there's Joanna Dennehy, but I didn't find her scary at all,' she told us. 'I was on the same block at

Bronzefield. We used to have exercise and stuff together. I thought she was pretty cold. She always attacked men. She always had men, didn't she? I was dying to speak to her. I always wanted to ask why she killed the dog, because she killed a couple of dog walkers and kept the dog. She said it was because the dog looked hungry so she kept the dog. I was dying to ask her that. She came to me in the changing room of the gym. She said, do you want some MDMA? And I thought, here's my chance.'

The picture she built was assembled at close range, over months. 'She's not how you'd imagine,' she told us. 'She's got a little Mohican, like a skinhead, absolute machine in the gym. Really, really petite. But rock-solid. She's a lesbian. I'm not sure if you've heard the story of her partner inside, Hayley Palmer. Hayley took her second name and everything.'

Yvonne had spent time researching Dennehy's case independently, having delivered a presentation on her as part of her criminology studies. 'I did my presentation on her,' she told us. 'She actually enjoyed it. She would have carried on. I think her goal was nine or ten, wasn't it? She wasn't done at three. She would have carried on. She was crazy.' She had met people who had been in close proximity to Dennehy, she added. 'She's had a girlfriend inside, you know, that girlfriend's come out now. She's set herself up. She was ruling the roost in there.'

It is a detail that stays with you. One of Britain's most dangerous women, architect of a killing spree that shocked the country, brought low by a spice habit and a relationship that ended in a pool of blood on a prison floor. Dennehy herself walked away. She always does.

But Joanna Dennehy was one thread in a larger picture. Neah described the institution itself with the same directness, and we must stress that this is her opinion.

'Bronzefield has a lot more corruption, a lot more relationships between staff and prisoners. The lines are so much more blurred and so much more out in the open than in a government prison. You're more likely to get away with certain things, and it's easier to get your hands on things. But the bang-up is a lot more, and it's harder to get legitimate things achieved, because it's like, one minute they want to bring you in a bottle of vodka, and the next you want an extra visit home. Where's the line?'

Her first night there was one she described with something close to gratitude for a single act of care. 'On my first night I came back from reception and a female officer called Paula was on duty,' she told us. 'She said, are you okay? I said I was. She said, I'm going to make sure you don't go to healthcare. I don't think it'll be good for you. She let me go back to my room. She probably stopped something bad happening that night. After a ten-year sentence coming through, you can imagine what some people might try and do.

'Then I called my mum. I'd told my family the wrong court dates because I didn't want anyone there. I didn't want to watch my family hurting while I was going through it. My mum was absolutely shocked. She couldn't believe it. I remember just sitting there all night, just in shock, because I'd never seen anything like that happen right in front of my eyes.'

Being classified as high risk imposed its own particular dynamic, she said. 'Because of my charge I was classified as high risk, so I was in a single cell at first, which after a while becomes unbearable. It's boring, but you also can't live with people for too long because they're not long-termers. So the minute you get the risk classification taken off and you can have a cellmate, you then have to get it put back on, because you can't just say, I was all right with them for a couple of months but now I can't share. You have to make them really believe you're a danger. A lot of times I'd get that classification up, get it put down again, and then have to demand it back. It's just a way of prison life.'

The mental health provision at Bronzefield was something she returned to. 'There are a lot of people in there who shouldn't be there,' she told us. 'A lot of mental health issues that are not understood or helped or supported. And of course being there makes it worse if you go in already unwell. I remember at Bronzefield there was a woman banging on the pipe all night, which is quite common. The pipes carry sound across the whole building. Everyone would be shouting, shut up, stop it. Come the morning, I found out she just wanted her medication. She'd been rude to a nurse earlier and they'd said, you're not getting it. They don't care; they're going home. She was mentally unwell and going to be in real distress all night.'

On the food, she was precise. 'The food at Bronzefield

was better in terms of edible, but it was a lot more processed, a lot of stuff in packets. At Holloway it was just anything chucked together. At Bronzefield you'd get packaged sandwiches and things. You're not allowed kettles at Bronzefield, they say because it's maximum security. So you can make noodles in a flask but that's about it. Every Saturday was fry-up day, a burger, fried egg, bacon. Every Friday, in every prison I've been in, fish and chip Friday. Everyone loves that. The food is really there to keep you fat, lazy and fatigued so you're more controllable. You realise that after a while.'

Yvonne had heard a similar account from a friend who had been held there. 'She said it was like the Wild West,' Yvonne told us. 'It felt like contrasting styles. She said a certain type of person prefers it, because you can get a lot more past them in terms of contraband, and it's much more easily corrupted. There are lots of dodgy staff – that was her take on the difference between the privately owned and the government prisons.'

Bronzefield was to receive much more interest in 2023, on receiving a notorious prisoner. Lucy Letby was born on 4 January 1990 in Hereford, the only child of John and Susan Letby. Her upbringing was comfortable and loving. She qualified as a children's nurse in 2011 and joined the neonatal unit at the Countess of Chester Hospital as a full-time nurse.

In 2015, the neonatal unit at the Countess of Chester Hospital began to record an unusual and disturbing rise in the number of unexplained infant deaths and serious collapses. The pattern was noted in July of that year, when it became apparent that Lucy Letby was the only nurse present at every one of the deaths that had taken place on the unit. Further deaths followed. By February 2016, common links across the incidents had been formally identified. Consultant paediatricians urged executives to remove Letby from the unit. By July 2016, under sustained pressure from clinical staff, she was finally moved to a clerical role. The unexpected collapses stopped.

Letby was arrested in 2018 and charged in November 2020 with seven counts of murder and 15 counts of attempted murder relating to 17 babies. Her trial began at Manchester Crown Court and lasted over ten months. On 18 August 2023, the verdict was delivered. Letby was found guilty of murdering seven babies and attempting to murder six more. She was sentenced to life imprisonment with a whole-life order. A retrial on a further count in July 2024 found her guilty of attempting to murder Child K. She was handed a 15th whole-life sentence. Letby chose not to attend the sentencing hearing in August 2023 and was therefore not present to hear the victim impact statements read aloud in court.

Since conviction, the case has attracted considerable controversy, including sustained criticism of the medical and scientific evidence presented by the prosecution. Letby's new defence team submitted an application to the Criminal Cases Review Commission. Both of her formal appeals against conviction were refused: the first by a single judge in January 2024, and the second, following a three-day hearing at the Court of Appeal in April 2024, by a panel comprising Dame Victoria Sharp, Lord Justice Holroyde and Mrs Justice Lambert, who concluded that the trial had been thoughtful, fair, comprehensive and correct. The Thirlwall Inquiry, hearing evidence through 2024 and into 2025, examined the failures that allowed the deaths at the Countess of Chester Hospital to go unaddressed for as long as they did. In 2025, former senior executives of the hospital were arrested on suspicion of gross negligence manslaughter. All were released on bail pending further investigation.

Letby was held at New Hall before her transfer to Bronzefield. Jo Taylor had contacts inside.

'Lucy Letby is in there,' Jo told us. 'My friends say she's not going to do things. She won't go to court. She went in civvies. Lucy Letby says what she wants. She is on a hospital ward for her own protection. Apparently she's very cocky, and pretty controlling. In the olden days you never refused a judge. Why not get her in a body belt and then put duct tape over her mouth? I would have Lucy Letby in there kicking and screaming. But human rights, you can't do it now.'

Vanessa placed the question of Letby's management within a longer arc that she had seen play out with other notorious prisoners. 'There will come a time down the line when Lucy Letby will be risk assessed regarding whether she can rejoin the general population,' she told us. 'The same happened with Rose West. Rose West was kept separate at Holloway and at Durham, but as the press died down and her reputation died down, she was re-risk assessed. Myra Hindley was working on receptions. She had a job and was back in the general population. At some point you have to rejoin them into society and the general population for their benefit. Keeping someone separate costs money and also isn't good long-term for someone's mental state.'

She was direct about the particular vulnerability of a child killer within the women's estate. 'Particularly with women, child killers are seen as the lowest of the low in the pecking order,' she said. 'The fact that a lot of women have had their children taken away from them because of their prison sentence, or may have lost babies or miscarried. When put in with someone who is a child killer, it can be very provocative and raw and bring a lot of emotions to the surface. There are a lot of lifers, doing life, the likes of Joanna Dennehy, who would absolutely delight in having the scalp of Lucy Letby. Without a doubt.'

Suzy had the most uncomfortable observation to make – one that had less to do with Letby than with the rest of us. 'She's a different kind of prisoner in the sense that people can't accept that she did what she did,' she said. 'Because she's a doe-eyed, middle-class girl. She doesn't come across as the sort of person you'd expect to have done what she's supposed to have done. I wonder whether there's an agenda that this can't possibly be true, because she seems such an ordinary kind of girl. Looking back to Rosemary West or Myra Hindley, there was a man involved in both cases, and I think there was more of an acceptance that the woman was in a secondary role to the man. This is a lone operator. No one to share the blame with. And for somebody like that, and in this social media age, the look of her doesn't help the case for her guilt. She looks quite sweet and innocent. They always find the picture that makes someone look like a crazed maniac. All the pictures you see of Lucy Letby, she's this sort of angelic-looking young woman. You'd be happy to sit next to her on the bus.'

Two hundred miles north, in West Yorkshire, is where Rose West lives. HMP New Hall, the source of media fascination for decades, given its notorious inmates.

CHAPTER 6

HMP New Hall

*'She was rude and obnoxious. People used to spit on
her from the top of the landing. She was chauffeured
around by the officers.'*
ANASTASIA SEVERN

A woman convicted of ten murders, making herself
useful in the kitchen, kept apart from most of the
other women, known on the wing by a different name.
That is what the system had made of Rosemary West,
and New Hall had held her long enough to observe the
shape of it.

HMP New Hall is a closed-category prison for female
adults, juveniles and young offenders, located in the
village of Flockton near Wakefield in West Yorkshire,
operated by His Majesty's Prison Service. New Hall
carries a longer and more colourful history than its current
role necessarily suggests. It opened in 1933 as the first
open prison in England and Wales, operating as a satellite
of HMP Wakefield and housing men nearing the end of
their sentences – a trust-based, low-security experiment in

which prisoners worked the camp grounds in agriculture and maintenance as preparation for release. In 1961 it became a Senior Detention Centre for young male offenders. It was redesignated in 1987 and has operated as a women's prison ever since, tucked behind trees on the edge of Flockton village, five miles east of Wakefield. You can drive around its perimeter and view it from various different angles. It might be the most beautiful setting of any women's prison, reached through winding Yorkshire country lanes and open fields. It is currently one of three establishments in the female estate authorised to hold restricted status prisoners, and can accommodate up to 381 women.

Its residential units include Rivendell, a 30-room en suite wing housing restricted status prisoners, women on the enhanced regime and women with personality disorders. Since its redesignation, New Hall has held some of the most scrutinised women in the British penal system. Rosemary West, convicted in November 1995 of ten murders and sentenced to whole-life imprisonment, has been held there since 2019 following earlier periods at Holloway, Durham and Bronzefield. New Hall also became the subject of sustained public controversy in 2018 when it was confirmed that Karen White, a convicted rapist who had transitioned and been placed in the women's estate, had sexually assaulted two female prisoners while being held there, prompting a review of the policy governing the placement of transgender prisoners across the women's estate.

Bev was among the first officers posted to New Hall when it made the transition to a women's prison. Her description of the place in those early days makes clear how provisional and improvised the whole thing felt.

'It was a boys' detention centre,' Bev told us. 'It was just changing over to the female estate when we got there. So there were only about ten inmates when we got there. It was good for a couple of weeks because there were more staff than inmates. It was old. It had been repainted, but that was about it. When you went in through the gates, you'd go into the admin area, where the governor and all the admin staff were. And then you'd get into the main prison, and it's called a corridor. It was a long corridor. We used to call it the M1 because it was that long. And then off there, there was your staff room and your little office where you booked in. Then you had another bit which was the centre, where you had your radios and all the important bits. Then you had dorms, and then three wings, double wings, and then another dorm at the end. And then right at the very top was a gate and then two cells where if they were naughty, they went into these cells. It wasn't very practical. And then another gate to get into the education centre, so it was quite cramped.'

The physical layout created security problems that had to be fixed early. 'As the building was then, the inmates who were segregated in those two cells at the top of the M1 were in a position where the other inmates going through to education were passing them contraband,' she said.

'The segregated ones were quite happy, getting what they wanted. So we dealt with that in the end. Got rid of that segregation unit. Built a proper one that had the facilities for the ones who really needed to be away from the others. The bad ones and the ones who were there for their own protection. We called them VPs, vulnerable prisoners.'

Eleanor Brown described her route to New Hall in vivid detail.

'When you first go there, you're in the first night centre,' she told us. 'It's not huge – about 48 cells. Quite a clean-looking wing. Blue lino flooring, freshly painted. Your metal bed as you walk in, little cupboard, table, TV, sink, and then a toilet behind a partition. You're on your own. You're only ever kept there for a maximum of two weeks while they decide where you go next.'

The move to the main wings was where the gap between first impressions and reality opened up: she encountered a typical dingy cell that conformed to the stereotype most of us imagine.

Rivendell, the restricted status and enhanced wing, was a different world again. 'Rivendell has about 36 women,' she told us. 'Some are service users with personality disorders on a two-year programme. Then you've got your restricted status prisoners – your Rose Wests, your terrorists. A couple of people who can't go in the main jail because they wouldn't survive. And then your low-maintenance prisoners, which is what I was. It's like a prison within a prison. You're selected to go there. And in those cells there's a private bathroom, your own shower, a bigger desk, a nicer wardrobe. Not massively different – still the same cell door. But cleaner. Quieter.'

Rose West has circulated widely through the British women's prison system since the mid-1990s.

Born on 29 November 1953 in Northam, Devon, the fifth of seven children, Rosemary Pauline West met Frederick West when she was 15 and he was 27 and already married with children.

The crimes of Fred and Rose West are, even by the standards of the cases described in this book, of an exceptional and horrifying nature. They murdered at least 12 young women and girls between 1967 and 1987, though the full extent of the killings may never be known. Charmaine West, Rose's own stepdaughter, was eight years old when she died, almost certainly at Rose's hands while Fred was in prison.

Rose West was tried alone at Winchester Crown Court in October and November 1995. On 22 November 1995, she was found guilty on all ten counts of murder with which she had been charged. She received a whole-life sentence.

Rose West was held at Holloway prior to her trial, and Vanessa, who was in charge of the segregation unit at the time, looked after her there for around six to eight weeks. She was clear-eyed about the gap between media portrayal and the person she spent those weeks managing.

'Her crimes were dreadful,' Vanessa told us. 'She was found guilty of murdering ten women, one of whom was her stepdaughter. The media portrays her as this very violent, very evil, psychopathic, very narcissistic, personality disordered person. When, in actual fact, I looked after her in the segregation unit at Holloway prior to her trial. Prison officers as a whole take these things with a pinch of salt. You have to in order to work with these people and be professional. The way sometimes the media portrays murderers, rapists, whatever – although the crimes are separate, and they are dreadful crimes, the actual person themselves: you'd think they'd have evil stamped on their forehead, which they actually don't.'

As a prisoner, the woman West turned out to be was not what anyone had been led to expect. 'Rose West was very quiet; she was very, what I would call, a thinker,' Vanessa said. 'You could tell she was forever thinking something. She was very able to apply herself to pretty much everything we asked of her. If we got her out to clean, she'd clean. She never caused us any angst in looking after her. She came out on a nightly basis for an hour to watch the TV, because she was down there for her own protection, not punishment. So we used to get her out for an hour or so every evening. She was what I'd call an easy prisoner to work with.'

Vanessa was working on the day that Fred West died. The task of telling Rose fell to the duty governor, who arrived at the segregation unit and asked Vanessa to open the cell door.

'I happened to be working,' she told us. 'I got a phone call from the communications room saying the duty governor was on the way down to see Rose West. When he came down he came into the office where I was sitting and he said, "I've got to tell Rose that her husband has committed suicide." I opened the cell door and Rose was sat on her bed reading and I said, "Rose, the governor's got something he wants to tell you," and she was like, "Oh right, yes." He said, "Rose, I'm really sorry to tell you that Fred, your husband, has committed suicide, and he was found just after lunch today in Winson Green prison." And all Rose said was, "Oh, okay then." That was it. No emotion, no nothing. This was allegedly the love of her life.'

She reflected afterwards on what that absence of reaction might mean. 'A bit of both,' she told us. 'I also think that she thought, as did Fred, if he topped himself she'd get off, and I think she firmly believed that. They say psychopaths have no emotion, and clearly she had no emotion. There was an absolute blankness there. She certainly knew what was happening; you could see that she acknowledged it and took it in, but she didn't show any emotion, which I always thought was strange.'

Her summary of West as a prisoner to manage was blunt and, in its way, instructive. 'She was no bother,' she told us. 'She is narcissistic and manipulative but she obeyed everyone, kept her head down, but she was very aware. When the papers jazz them up to be personified as evil, to me that just makes them something bigger than they actually are. At the end of the day, when you're in jail you're in jail. It doesn't matter who you are or what you've done.'

Geoffrey Wansell saw West's situation clearly when we asked him about her. 'Rosemary West is like Levi Bellfield: they realise full well they are very unlikely to ever be released from prison and they make the best of it,' he told us. 'But what do we as a society really have in mind? Is it an eye for an eye? The victim's families have every right to want revenge and retribution. We as a society have set our face against capital punishment, and I agree, but what then is the deterrent to the ultimate crime?'

On the question of release, Geoffrey was unambiguous. 'Rosemary West is exceptional, one of those cases, like Myra Hindley, where society could not bear for them to be released into society. We say people can be rehabilitated but I accept that she is the exception.'

Jo had come close to West more than once during her years at New Hall, without ever quite meeting her. The nearest she got was a budgie.

'Rose West changed her name to Jennifer Jones in Durham,' Jo told us. 'I saw her pet bird in her cell there but not her. Lifers in those days were entitled to budgies. They would have a budgie as a pet. I don't think they have that any more. This was the late 1990s. I would have liked to have seen Rose West. It was just a regular cell.'

Suzy had a more intimate view. She knew what Rose West's daily life actually looked like, and the picture was not what anyone might expect.

'Rose West goes by a different name now,' she told us. 'She is so terrified of exposure that she just wants to get her head down and for people not to know who she is.

She knows that is how life will be for her now. She lives on her wing and if she can just get up and go about her day, she knows where her limitations are. We've never heard a bad thing about her in terms of conduct inside prison. She does cookery, she's become quite a mumsy figure. If you passed her on the corridor, you wouldn't imagine what she was involved in. She's shuffling around in slippers. In every sense, she's tried to reinvent herself. Maybe that's the only way through it for her.'

One source who wished to remain anonymous had another fascinating anecdote about Rose West. She had gone to see West at a remand centre and explained that it would take some time before she could mix with the other women, and that in the meantime they needed to keep her occupied. We were curious to know what West wanted to do. 'She liked embroidery,' the source said. 'And then she said, "I want to do a landscape gardening course." And how I kept my face straight, I will never know. And then at Christmas, she got a Christmas cracker. And she got a skeleton key ring.'

Yvonne had spoken to a woman who had been on a wing with someone who knew West directly. 'She said she'd sat with Rose West,' Yvonne told us. 'She's now called Jennifer Jones or something. And everyone I met who was near her says she's nice. They call her auntie, don't they?'

Anastasia's account of West at New Hall gave us a typically open and blunt view. She had worked on the same wing, passed her on the landing. 'I saw Rose West,' she told us. 'She was rude and obnoxious. People used to spit on her from the top of the landing. She was chauffeured around by the officers.'

The picture Anastasia described – of a woman who attracted active hostility from the general population and required a protective escort to move around – sits alongside the quieter portrait offered by those who knew her more closely. The truth of West's daily life at New Hall likely contained both.

A woman who had been on Rivendell towards the end of her sentence experienced this proximity without warning. Eleanor, who served time at New Hall when sentenced, was allocated to the enhanced wing for her final weeks. She was three rooms along from West.

'In the main jail nobody likes the women on the enhanced wing. Nobody. I get that. But when you've been in that environment yourself, it gets really conflicted in your own head. Because you're like, I should really hate this person. But there's no benefit in walking around with animosity. It just holds you back. Rosemary West who was on that wing is very slight – slim build, skinny legs but with a stomach. She just wears leggings, grey shorts. She shuffles around. She does cookery. She's become quite a mumsy figure. If you passed her on the corridor, you would not imagine what she was involved in. She wasn't what I expected at all.'

On the question of how other women on the wing regarded West, Eleanor was direct. 'The women in the main jail – they hate her. But anyone who's actually been around her – they just say leave it. She is no bother. And when I was joking with one of the officers about it, he said to me – I understand why you couldn't drop it, but she's actually all right. She's valid. That was the general feeling among the staff who knew her.'

What Eleanor had not anticipated was the conversation that took place the night before her release.

'She came to my door,' Eleanor told us. 'She said to me, *"I want to give you a bit of advice. If you end up with a bad man, then run away from that man and run to the police. Wherever you're going, whatever you do, I hope you don't come back here."* I was stunned. I said no, no – I don't intend to. It was just surreal. That was advice she was giving me! At the end of the day, that was a human being who came to my door and said, you don't want to spend the rest of your life the way I did and don't make the mistakes I did.'

Her account of West was not what most people would expect from someone who had spent weeks three doors along from one of Britain's most notorious killers. It was more complicated than hatred, and more honest than sympathy. 'My understanding of that killer couple and those crimes is that Fred West was the main person, and she went along with it and became part of it. But I don't let Rose West off the hook – I think she should have done way more to stop those crimes. She followed somebody terrible, and got sucked in. And I think that's what a lot of women do . . . but it doesn't change what happened. You don't want to spend the rest of your life like that.'

She also told us about the dynamics between Dennehy and West – a detail she had heard from those who were on the wing when both were held there. 'She hates men,' she said of Dennehy. 'Yeah. She likes women. But not Rose. Apparently, her and Rose have a history. So I don't know whether Rose wants to kill her or she wants to kill Rose. Because there's something bad there. I did hear that if a male officer tries to get involved with her she's kicking off.' She told us about one prisoner she had become close to. 'I really liked her. We got on really well. She literally laid it all out in front of me, what happened to her. She's just an ordinary person, but she's not quiet about the fact that she killed a man. When they were both taking cocaine, it just heated up, and then she stabbed him. How do you put a knife in someone? It used to scare me, listening to her. She explained that it is like . . . one second . . . only a moment. She says, like, she remembered stuff and just being stood over his body, thinking *What have I done?* And that happened within two or three seconds. And you can see how you can get to that point. I'm not a feminist in the sense that I say women are perfect and men aren't, but you must see that a lot of the women in there, their crime is aggravated by men.'

She told us about a phone call with her grandfather that had stayed with her. 'My grandad, God bless him. I was on the phone with him when I was in jail. I've grown up with him . . . I can do no wrong in my grandad's eyes. And when I was in prison, he said to me, "Can I ask you something?" Because he can never understand it. I said, "Yeah, of course." "Have you hurt anyone?" I said, "No, I've not hurt anyone, Grandad." Because he can't get his head around it. Because he thinks they are the people that society needs to be protected from, like, that's the last resort, like, to go to prison. I used to wake up in the morning inside and like feel really bad and convince myself that I was someone who deserved to be in there. That I've done something to justify why I'm waking up in prison. What's going on? How is this happening?'

She had followed the Letby case and had views on it based on her conversations with other prisoners. 'The more I hear about the case, the more I think she did it.'

★ ★ ★

Karen Matthews staged the kidnapping of her own daughter Shannon in 2008 in a scheme designed to claim reward money. Shannon was found hidden in the base of a divan bed at the home of Michael Donovan, the uncle of Karen's then-boyfriend Craig Meehan, less than a mile from the family's house in Dewsbury Moor, West Yorkshire, 24 days after her disappearance. She was unharmed but had been drugged and tethered during her captivity, tests later revealing she had been routinely sedated for months before her disappearance.

Shannon and her siblings were taken into care. Matthews was convicted and sentenced to eight years. She was released in April 2012, having served approximately four years, and given a new surname to protect her safety.

Matthews was held on the segregation unit at New Hall, and Nicola Webster had spent time with her there every day.

'The only person that I can say really sticks in my mind is Karen Matthews,' Nicola told us. 'I used to see her every day on the segregation unit. She's the only one that when the telly was on and she was on the news – she never mentioned it once. But I think she's got learning difficulties, and it wasn't all about that. I think she was manipulated herself. She was vulnerable. She was on the segregation because of that. And of course, that's another part of the prison now, isn't it? – vulnerable wings, vulnerable people, whether they've got learning difficulties, it's a high-profile case or whatever it is.'

The trial judge had noted doubts about whether Matthews could have conceived the Shannon kidnapping scheme unaided. The serious case review described her as having been assessed with a borderline learning disability on two separate occasions before the offence. What Nicola remembered, sitting with her every day on the segregation unit, was a woman who watched herself on the television news and said nothing.

Juli Flintoff arrived at New Hall shortly after being married, posted there without prior knowledge of the place and was thrown in at the deep end on her first shift.

'My first day was overwhelming,' she told us. 'I started at Wakefield Prison doing a summer school. I didn't know that New Hall existed. New Hall seemed totally different to Wakefield. A long corridor. I had only been married a week. Did I have a mentor? Nobody. E Wing was relatively new, for experienced officers. My first shift was on the mother and baby unit. I was thrown in at the deep end. My posting was E Wing. There were nine on my course and I was the only one down there. I was on the other two wings. They call you newbie.'

The lifers at New Hall had done many years at Durham first, she said, and all of that had been dealt with by the time they arrived. They were trying to get to Askham Grange. 'New Hall had a second-stage lifer system,' she told us. 'They came from Durham, down to us at New Hall, then on to an open prison after jumping through hoops. They had specially trained officers who worked with them.'

What she carried from her years there was an image of the place's particular darkness. 'Women's prison is a very dark place. The smell of puke and diarrhoea from people coming off drugs. Dark and dingy. Not much light coming through the bars. I did my job and I did it well.'

Kay Lumb transferred to New Hall as control room and surveillance instructor, arriving in the early days when the prison was still adjusting to its new population.

'We arrived and we didn't have any prisoners,' she told us. 'We were almost grieving the lack of prisoners. The first few months were spent training staff. We retained some male staff across the service. Not everyone is suitable for a cross-sex posting. Female staff working in male prisons – some of them, if a male prisoner was flirting, they didn't handle it in the proper manner. Some male staff saw female prisoners as female instead of prisoners. Prisoners have an ability to seek your weaknesses out.'

One of the stranger memories from those early years was a royal visit. 'Princess Diana opened up the F Wing,' Kay told us. 'There was a plaque. That disappeared. In Flockton, the village where New Hall is, there is a special school. I got the special needs kids in once a week on Thursday. They loved it. Only one occasion when a prisoner said these should have been put down at birth. One student, Sarah, she was in a wheelchair. She gave Princess Diana a bouquet of flowers she had and Princess Diana took them.'

It was intelligence from a trusted prisoner – the same incident, and the same Gillian, that opened this book – that had once prevented a serious incident on the wing. 'The last thing any prisoner wants is to be known as a grass,' Kay told us. 'She said, I'm just going off the wing for a second. She said, there's a knife in the bed on the wing; it's meant for a certain officer. Gillian had made the knife. They had plastic cutlery. She'd got a piece of wooden handle off a gardening tool and had strapped something like a leather shoelace and wrapped the handle of the knife with it.'

'When I first started at New Hall, there weren't many drug patients,' Nicola told us. 'There wasn't heroin and cocaine and all these other things to the extreme that there is now. When it first started to become a problem, they opened a wing, and that wing was the detox wing, and then it got bigger. Whereas now, I think you've potentially got 95 per cent of the prison population actually on a detox.'

At New Hall, as across the English estate, the experience of women in custody is shaped by a system that was designed for men and has never been adequately remade. Across the border, a different approach has been taking shape for the better part of two decades.

CHAPTER 7

Scotland, Northern Ireland & Wales

'We can do everything with the individual, but if community and society don't change, they see the person that went in, not the person that comes out.'
STEPHEN HILLIS

Scotland, Northern Ireland and Wales each have their own prison services, their own inspectorates, their own legal frameworks, and in Scotland's case their own increasingly distinctive ideas about what custody is supposed to achieve. For women in particular, the distance between what happens north of the border and what happens in England is striking and growing.

The history of women's imprisonment in each of the three nations runs deeper than the institutions currently holding them. Before Cornton Vale opened in 1975, Scottish women were held across local prisons in Greenock, Edinburgh, Perth and Aberdeen, dispersed and largely invisible to any central oversight. In Northern Ireland, women were held for most of the 20th century at HMP

Armagh, the Victorian prison at the centre of Armagh city whose history became bound up with the internment of Republican prisoners during the Troubles, the 1980 dirty protest, and persistent dispute over strip-searching and conditions. Women were moved from Armagh to Mourne House at Maghaberry in 1986, and then again to Ash House at Hydebank Wood in 2004. Wales does not have a dedicated women's prison. Welsh women have served their sentences in English establishments since the emergence of a modern custodial system, at distances that for many of them exceed 100 miles from home.

The question of which women Scotland has held at the most serious end of its estate has been shaped in recent years as much by policy controversy as by individual cases. Avril Jones was convicted alongside her partner Edward Cairney in June 2019 of the murder of Margaret Fleming, a 19-year-old with learning disabilities whose absence went unreported for 17 years; Jones had fraudulently claimed benefits in Fleming's name throughout. Isla Bryson, convicted of raping two women in 2016 and 2019 prior to transition and remanded briefly to Cornton Vale in early 2023, ignited urgent debate in the Scottish Parliament and prompted a national political crisis before being swiftly moved. Tiffany Scott, held for years in segregation and described by prison staff as the most dangerous prisoner in the Scottish system, moved between institutions each of which eventually declared it could not manage her; she was taken ill at HMP Grampian on the night of 28 February 2024 and died at

Aberdeen Royal Infirmary the following day, her death treated as unexplained by Police Scotland. In Northern Ireland, the separated prisoners at Hydebank – women who identify as Republican paramilitary prisoners and do not recognise the authority of the Northern Ireland Prison Service – represent a category without parallel anywhere else in the British estate.

For almost half a century, that course ran through Cornton Vale. HMP and YOI Cornton Vale was a purpose-built women's prison and young offenders institution in Stirling, opened in 1975, and for most of its life it was a byword for institutional failure. A 2012 review conducted by former Lord Advocate Elish Angiolini described it as a miserable place where conditions were antediluvian and appalling. Eleven women killed themselves there between 1995 and 2002. When inspectors visited in 2019 they found deeply vulnerable women in need of urgent psychiatric care. One woman had bitten through the skin and muscle of her arm to the bone, and another had set her hair on fire.

Scotland's response to Cornton Vale's accumulated failures took a different form from the originally proposed large replacement prison near Greenock. Instead, Scotland adopted a smaller-facilities model, building a new national establishment on the site of the closed Cornton Vale and opening two Community Custody Units, the first of their kind anywhere in the United Kingdom. HMP and YOI Stirling opened in June 2023, designed by Holmes Miller and built by Morrison Construction at a cost of

£85.7 million. The prison has a design capacity of 117, with a separate mother and baby unit providing two further spaces. It was built as a deliberate rejection of everything Cornton Vale looked like. There are no bars on windows. Residential areas are arranged in single-storey houses around a central garden. The eight units are named after flowers chosen by women from across the estate.

Cornton Vale closed in April 2023, its remaining population dispersed across the estate before the move to Stirling. Women entering the new prison are assessed there and transferred to other parts of the estate according to their needs and risk profile. The aim is to move them as quickly as possible towards the least restrictive setting appropriate to them.

In 2026, women in Scotland can be held in secure custody at four locations beyond the two Community Custody Units. HMP and YOI Stirling is the national reception and assessment centre. HMP Grampian, near Peterhead in the north-east, holds women in a dedicated female hall alongside its male population and has its own mother and baby unit. HMP Greenock manages women in Darroch Hall and Bute House, a mix of short-term convicted and untried prisoners. HMP Polmont, historically a young offenders institution for males, now also holds adult women transferred from other establishments. HMP Edinburgh, which appears in older accounts of the female estate, no longer holds women at all; they were moved when Stirling opened.

The Bella Centre in Dundee's Hilltown opened in

August 2022 with 16 places across three shared houses. The Lilias Centre, in Glasgow's Maryhill, opened two months later with capacity for 24. Together they hold a maximum of 40 women. Both were the first of their kind anywhere in the United Kingdom and both have drawn international attention. The original Scottish government plan, announced in 2015, envisaged five Community Custody Units across Scotland. Only two had been built at the time of writing, with the remaining three pending the outcome of an evaluation of how the model was working. A University of Glasgow-led study published in December 2025, commissioned by the Scottish government, drew on interviews with 33 women living in the CCUs and 48 staff. Women spoke positively about their accommodation and their access to healthcare and said they felt safe. But researchers warned there was a real danger that the units had become, as they put it, mini prisons, retaining many features of traditional incarceration and falling short of the radical departure first envisaged.

Wendy Sinclair-Gieben spent years as a prison governor in England, Scotland and Australia before becoming HM Chief Inspector of Prisons for Scotland. She led inspections of HMP Stirling and both Community Custody Units and had thought carefully about what had been achieved and what had not. She was precise about the history and direct about its limitations.

She explained how the Corston Report in England had already identified that women did better in smaller community settings closer to home, and how Scotland had reached the same conclusion through the Angiolini Inquiry. The prison rules in Scotland, she noted, still applied to women, children and adult men in precisely the same way, which she regarded as the central unresolved failure of the reform programme.

'There was a report commissioned by Elish Angiolini which identified that there were five areas in Scotland that would benefit from having small, discrete community custody units,' she said, 'because culturally, women are different to men when they're in prison. They need to be in touch with their families. They still take primary care responsibility. And the proportion of women who have identified neurodiverse issues and abuse issues is much, much higher than it is in the male estate.'

We asked about the provision for women in Scotland who required high secure forensic mental healthcare. There was no facility in the country capable of providing it, she told us. 'For forensic mental health patients, if they need high secure, they are sent to Rampton,' she said. 'There is no high secure place for women in Scotland. Carstairs, the local secure forensic estate, does have the space. But they argue that it varies between one and three women, and they're not going to open up a ward and staff a unit for between one and three women.'

The failure to change the prison rules alongside the physical infrastructure was the battle she had fought hardest and got furthest nowhere with. But she described one achievement that clearly meant a great deal to her. 'I harassed the Cabinet Secretary and succeeded in getting all children removed from prison in Scotland,' she said. 'That went through in legislation just as I was leaving.' Legislation enacted under the Children (Care and Justice) (Scotland) Act 2024 means that no one under 18 can now be remanded or sentenced to a young offenders institution in Scotland.

Wendy described the Community Custody Units in terms that made plain both their novelty and the constraints that still bound them. 'They have five-foot fences around the edge, which could easily be jumped over,' she said. 'They're set in nice surroundings with plants and trees. They're little houses holding six women, sometimes fewer where there are disabled adaptations. They've got their own sitting rooms, their own kitchens, and everybody has an en suite bedroom. There are communal areas for meetings and groups and courses. Healthcare is run by the local NHS trust. There are no uniforms. The women can wear what clothes they want.'

The 2011 prison rules, she said, were the thing that stopped the CCUs being everything they were supposed to be. 'They're still having to abide by the old-fashioned 2011 prison rules, which were designed for men. So quite often women arrive and it takes a long time for them to achieve the benchmark needed to be allowed to go into the community. But the concept was that they would go into the community for work, do their own shopping, cook for themselves. It's very impressive.' She spoke with evident pride in this radical new concept. 'The Lilias and the Bella do not look like prisons. They look like little cottages around a circle. The local community doesn't even realise they're prisons.'

We asked where she would direct someone wanting to understand both sides of the model. She was clear. 'I would definitely do Lilias,' she said, 'but then I'd also go and have a look at Polmont. You could go and look at Stirling, which is the women's prison, and you'll be impressed with it.' Something had struck her on inspection. 'Stirling's got about a hundred women,' she said. 'So if it was a hundred men, you would have a big gym, wouldn't you? A hundred women, they have a small room. I thought: this is stereotypical architecture.'

On where the model needed to go next, she was specific. 'The only complaint I have with the CCUs is they need to go a bit further and do what some of the American women's prisons do,' she said, 'allow children to stay overnight before the women go out. Because having not had to deal with children and then going out and suddenly having to deal with them is tough. A lot of play therapy, learning to handle your kids, putting them to bed, making meals for them, knowing what to do to be a good parent: these are things we don't do well. They come and visit for a couple of hours and that's it, whereas they should be able to have their children for a weekend, especially in the CCUs, because they don't look like prisons.'

The question of why Scotland had moved so decisively in this direction while England had largely not was one she had turned over many times. 'They've also developed a new system of control and restraint, the approach used for violent and difficult prisoners, which they're rolling out across all the prisons, and it doesn't require pain compliance,' she said. 'Every prison in England still uses pain compliance, apart from the juvenile estate.' And then to something deeper. 'Scotland has a different culture to England. It has roughly the same population as Yorkshire. But it has a much closer engagement with ministers. There isn't an intervening Ministry of Justice standing between the staff and whoever. As a prison governor, you are likely to meet the ministers. The relationship is very close and very different.'

She was not simply a cheerleader for the Scottish system. 'Polmont is hugely overcrowded and is not run on therapeutic lines,' she said. 'But they do try to move people through to the more therapeutic prisons as fast as possible.' And on the gap between the rhetoric of reform and the front-line reality, she added: 'Scotland has often led the way in enlightened thinking. You'll remember Barlinnie had a special unit: Jimmy Boyle, all of that. But sometimes the rhetoric doesn't filter its way down to what the women actually experience.'

Scotland does not operate a whole-life tariff in the form used in England and Wales. What it has instead is the Order for Lifelong Restriction, under which a person is assessed every year. When it was introduced, the expectation was that perhaps 15 or 20 people would ever receive one. By the time of writing, around 200 were subject to an OLR. Whether any woman had ever been given one was something Wendy could not confirm from her own experience of the estate. 'I've met all the women in the Scottish prisons over the last few years, every single one,' she said, 'and I haven't come across anyone with an OLR who's been in for 27 years and is unlikely to get out.'

On sentencing more broadly she was emphatic, drawing on decades of observation. 'There's a lot of evidence to support the idea that female violence is judged much more harshly than male violence,' she said. 'Likewise, for BAME people: they get much longer, stronger sentences. The stop and search statistics say it all.' She described cases that illustrated the point. A woman with a gun licence standing on her own farm telling road builders they were not coming on to her land. A single mother in Wales who stole school uniforms because there was no second-hand scheme in place when the local authority introduced a new uniform policy, and whose children the magistrates were intent on having adopted. A woman accused of starting a fire in which her children died, who turned out to be innocent – who had a baby on the way to hospital and was returned to the prison while the baby went on without her, who had a massive nervous breakdown and a ruptured relationship with the rest of her family, and whose story had since been the subject of a television documentary. And a woman who had smashed cars when drunk, spent two years on bail getting her life together, attending Alcoholics Anonymous, holding down a job, never having harmed a person, and who was then sent to prison for three months by a different sheriff who simply paid no attention to what the previous one had arranged. Her children went into care.

'What's interesting is I know a fair number of sheriffs, and they are absolutely divided,' she said. 'Some believe wholeheartedly that drug courts, family courts, deferred sentencing, problem-solving courts are all beneficial and effective. And then you've got others who say bang them up, lock them up and throw away the key.'

Most of the women she had encountered, she said, had no business being in prison at all. 'The level of acquired brain injury, the level of undocumented abuse. Quite often the crimes were nasty, heinous at times. But an awful lot of it could have been prevented at a much earlier age.'

What she had encountered on her inspection rounds she returned to with a kind of contained feeling. She recalled a young woman of 17 who had found herself entirely alone in the system, with no one else in the prison anywhere near her age. 'She felt completely isolated, completely alone, away from her family. She was despairing,' she said. 'But the staff were wonderful. One played pool with her. One went and got her a cup of tea. One said, let's get you into the hairdresser. Just making an effort to make her feel safe and cared for. When I went back to see her a couple of weeks later, because I was worried about her, she was just coping. She'd moved into that transition of: "I can manage this."'

During the same inspection period she had encountered two other women whose situations gave her pause. One had come from a medium secure psychiatric hospital and had arrived in prison convinced it was better. We asked her to say more. 'She said, "this prison is so different,"' Wendy told us. '"People treat you with respect. I'm listened to, I've got time on my own. Whereas the medium secure facility I was in was truly appalling in comparison."' Wendy had put it to her that perhaps the treatment of the illness that had put her in hospital was what she was actually experiencing differently. 'She said, "oh, no, some of the staff in here are truly awful and they're corrupt," the woman had replied. '"But on the whole, the atmosphere is one of respect. Whereas in the medium secure psychiatric hospital it was not an attitude of respect. It was an attitude of control."' Wendy was struck by that. 'I thought, well, that is interesting,' she said.

She recalled too a woman in her forties with the mental age of a young child who should never have been in prison at all, and around whom the other women had quietly organised themselves in ways that had nothing to do with any official programme. 'I was walking around with the governor and she came running up and said, "will you dance with me?"' Wendy recalled. 'And the governor said, "yes, of course I will." I just thought: wow. The staff had done a reasonable amount to try to keep her occupied and happy. But the other prisoners had clubbed together and were teaching her dances, teaching her the words to pop songs, just making her life okay, even though she was clearly very vulnerable. Seriously impressive.'

During the inspection of HMP Stirling and both

Community Custody Units, Wendy had found herself in the company of nine elderly nuns, imprisoned as a result of the Scottish Child Abuse Inquiry into the institutions where they had worked with children. On the question of who should bear the cost of their imprisonment, she was direct. 'As a taxpayer, if you've got nuns who abuse children,' she said, 'then let the Catholic Church put them on house arrest and make them wear a tag and they're not allowed out. And the Catholic Church pays for them. Why should I?' She was also, she said, unsure how to handle their questions. 'It's a bit odd to be in a prison with a whole pile of elderly nuns,' she said. 'At one point one of them said, "why am I here?" And I thought, bugger it, I'll just play it up. I said, "God's will: you should be in here to help sort out the other women." She went, "I never thought of that." And I'm not religious at all. But it was the right thing to say.'

Tiffany Scott, a transgender prisoner who became one of the most discussed figures in the Scottish prison estate before her death in custody in February 2024, was someone Wendy spoke about with care. 'She was managed consistently in isolation because she was so dangerous,' she said. 'She would attack staff or other prisoners, and herself. She would pull bits out of herself, bite bits off and throw them at the staff. Horrendous. But I had a human rights colleague with me when I went to see her, and the staff were saying they'd stay with us. I said, no, it's fine. My colleague was absolutely terrified because of what he'd heard the staff saying. But as always, she was calm, delightful to talk to, really lovely. I brought her a cup of tea and a biscuit, had one myself, and it was an easy, pleasant conversation. She moved from prison to prison as each one felt it couldn't cope with her any more. I just felt for her.'

The emotional weight of those encounters was something Wendy had carried for years. We asked whether the work with women had taken more from her than the work with men. 'I prefer managing men,' she said. 'Because it's simpler, it's much, much simpler. I tended to get wrapped up in the women and get distressed by them. So when you see a child being plucked off its mother because the mother has to go back and the child doesn't want to leave. And you know all the truisms, which is that men get a lot of visits from their children. Women don't, unless their mother brings them or the social services bring them. Wives always bring the kids to keep the husband going.' She described a case that had stayed with her. 'I always remember quite a young girl who was taken to Glastonbury by her mum and sold, sold for sex,' she said. 'And by the time she came into prison, some years later, she had been sold and sold and sold. And she was in a dreadful state, absolutely dreadful state. And she eventually committed suicide. I don't blame her. She really couldn't cope with what had happened to her. Being in prison, and it not happening to her, made her realise that life could be different. And as hard as we all worked with her to say, it can be like this in the community, it won't be like that, we can help you get there – she just couldn't cope with it. And I thought: that's your decision. I need to validate your decision rather than feeling incredibly bad that somehow I didn't stop you.' She paused. 'I found the emotional toll of working with women very, very tough. Very tough. So I prefer working with men.'

The estate Scotland has built over the past decade is the most deliberately designed women's custodial estate attempted anywhere in the United Kingdom. Northern Ireland has one prison. One site. Every woman in the jurisdiction ends up there.

HMP Hydebank Wood, formally known as Hydebank Wood College and Women's Prison, shares its grounds in South Belfast with a Young Offenders Centre holding young male prisoners aged 18 to 24. The female unit, Ash House, opened in June 2004 following extensive refurbishment and has a normal capacity of 86 women. Murray House, a smaller unit which sits outside the main walls but remains within the grounds, opened in 2015. Women there live under minimal security, able to work in local communities and move towards release. The consequence of a single facility for an entire jurisdiction is that every woman prisoner, regardless of where she came from or how far her family has to travel, ends up at this one site in Belfast. It is a constraint the prison cannot resolve, and it sits at odds with everything else the establishment has tried to become.

Hydebank was not always the place it is today. A 2013 inspection described it as failing, on a downward spiral, and identified more than 150 areas requiring improvement. Some inspectors argued publicly that the women should simply be moved, that Hydebank was the wrong environment for them. In 2016, the prison made national headlines when a female prisoner got pregnant after having sexual contact with a young man from the adjacent Young Offenders Centre, throwing into sharp relief just how porous the separation between the two populations could be. Supervision arrangements were tightened significantly in the aftermath.

The transformation since 2013 has, by most independent measures, been remarkable. By 2024, both parts of Hydebank had received full marks from inspectors, the first prison in Northern Ireland to achieve such a result. Justice Minister Naomi Long described it as a model of excellence and good practice. Over 90 per cent of those in custody were engaged in education, skills and work, and more than 600 certificates of achievement had been awarded in the preceding year alone.

Stephen Hillis had worked in learning and skills across the Northern Ireland Prison Service for eight years, first as Head of Learning and Skills at Hydebank and then as strategic lead across all three of the service's establishments: Maghaberry, Magilligan and Hydebank Wood. 'I happened to have a gap in my diary,' he told us, 'and went in, did some work at a resettlement prison in Nottinghamshire. That kind of lit the fire.' Prison was also in the family. His uncle had been a prison officer at Wandsworth. His grandfather had been a prison officer at Crumlin Road Gaol and had been present at the final hanging in Belfast. His mother had grown up in one of the houses on the Crumlin Road. Stephen described himself, with some amusement, as the tree-hugging hippie of the family.

'We are more than happy to broadcast what's happening inside, because not many people realise it,' he said. 'One of our big challenges is that we can do everything with the individual, but if community and society don't change, they see the person that went in, not the person that comes out.'

The full title of the establishment, he pointed out, was Hydebank Wood Women's Prison and Secure College. There was no HMP designation on it. The officers did not wear uniforms, a decision taken when the prison moved to a secure college model, and one he regarded as a marker of the whole philosophy. 'When you walk into the learning and skills centre, the whole premise is: do you feel like you're coming into a college?' he said. 'It has the college branding. The officers are there, but they're not in uniform. That's one of the main reasons. To foster that impression.' The physical transformation of the learning environment had been as significant as the philosophical one. He remembered what the classrooms had once looked like: cages outside them, a sight that had not alarmed anyone in Northern Ireland at the time, he noted drily, because that was what pubs and shops had looked like too. The contrast with what stood there now was a measure of how far the place had travelled.

The learning model itself had been rebuilt from first principles. 'You cannot mandate people to education, because education has failed these people in the past,' he said. 'You have to engage them. The strapline and mantra we use is: right student, right class, right time. Because if you get those three right, the individual gets a better outcome. If the timing's wrong, it fails everybody, including the other students in the classroom who are there at the right time.' They had taken away the must, he said. That had been a significant piece of work, perhaps six years earlier. The last thing you did with someone who arrived carrying significant addiction issues or in the grip of a psychotic episode was put them in a classroom. We asked about peer support. It was central to the model, he told us – peer learning, mentor support, strong engagement with speech and language therapy, because special educational needs across the estate were substantial and consistently under-recognised. 'Those would be the key areas,' he said, 'and I don't think they'll ever change as our priorities, quite frankly, because it's an ongoing process.'

He spoke about the physical environment at Hydebank. The female gardens were, he said, gorgeous, really well kept, a secure space with no males present unless officers were there, a bit of a sanctuary. There was a hair and beauty salon on the ground floor. A joinery workshop, painting and decorating, and light vehicle maintenance were available to both men and women, and was being snapped up by more and more of the women, which he said was great. Animal husbandry had been a feature for years. There were donkeys and sheep. There had been pygmy goats until they started headbutting people's shins.

The main kitchen served the entire population of the establishment, but working in it required a Level 2 qualification in Catering and Hospitality. A teacher worked alongside the women there every day. The Cabin, a cafe run within the prison, required every woman working there to complete her barista and customer service qualifications first. 'If everybody stopped drinking coffee in the world, we'd stop delivering barista training,' he said, 'because it has to be related to job opportunities on the outside.'

Murray House, the pre-release unit beyond the main walls, held five or six women at a time and had been running for around 11 years, born out of the crisis moment when the decision had to be made whether Hydebank could be saved at all. Stephen described what it was designed to do, and what happened when the gap between custody and the outside world turned out to be wider than expected. One woman he had known from his time there had a simple ambition when she finally got out for work: she wanted a Big Mac. 'She walked into McDonald's, saw the big touch screens, panicked, went outside, burst into tears, came back, and said she needed to go back in,' he recalled. 'From our point of view, that's a massive learning piece. The world has moved so far, even in three or four years, and this lady hadn't been out in 12 or 13 years.'

The problem of skills becoming obsolete over a long sentence is a real one. The question of how to pace education across a long sentence was one he took seriously. If the prison gave a lifer the full range of skills within the first five years of a 17-year sentence, those skills would be irrelevant by the time of release. The answer was a bespoke approach and close collaboration with the wider prison leadership.

We asked about the particular challenges of engaging women in education. Stephen was direct. 'Engaging females in education is more difficult than males,' he said. 'For many, because it's building employability capacity, they go: I'm not going back to work, I'm going back to the community; I'm going to look after my kids. So we have to provide a different hook.' He described the approach with women from the travelling community, for whom the idea of female education carried a specific cultural resistance. 'We have a lot of travellers, as you can imagine, where education for females is just a no-no culturally,' he said. 'Do you want to be the pioneer for that? Because look how that's worked out for you. And it is those frank conversations: why would you not take a different approach, because the approach up to now – well, you're sitting here talking to us.'

On the difference between how men and women experienced longer sentences, he was considered. 'The females are more cerebral about it,' he said. 'Guys can hunker down and just go, right, this is what's happening today, I'll survive today to get through to the next day. Whereas I do feel a lot of our female students – I would call them students, but prisoners – would be trying to run a normal life. They're still a mum, they're still a grandmum, they're still an aunt. It's a strange juxtaposition.'

We asked about the make-up of the population. Around 50 per cent were on remand, he said – but that figure included long-term remand, since some women made a pragmatic calculation. 'Some people go: I'm going to be here, so I might as well do the time now,' he said. We noted that for some women, custody appeared to offer a stability unavailable outside. He acknowledged it with some ambivalence. 'It also, unfortunately, can be a safe haven for some women as well,' he said. 'So, we do have returners.'

One aspect of Hydebank that carried no parallel elsewhere in the British women's estate was the presence of separated prisoners: women who identified as Republican paramilitary prisoners and did not accept the authority of the Northern Ireland Prison Service. At the time of the interview there were two such women on a dedicated landing, with their own staff and their own routines, entirely apart from the rest of the population. 'They see themselves as prisoners of war,' Stephen said. 'That's the language that's used. I can't just rock up to their landing as I would with the others. It has to be cleared, and they have to agree to it. We talk and we offer opportunities. But more often than not, they don't engage.'

On the outcomes for the women who came through Hydebank, he was honest about the full range. There were women who had gone on to lead in their communities, to really make a difference, to face the world that had distorted their lives and meet it head-on. And there were those who had not. 'Others have fallen back. Others simply haven't made it,' he said. 'And that's probably the hardest thing, particularly when you see it reported somewhere: somebody that your teachers and staff worked with, that you thought, yes, yes, yes.'

'There's been a real evolution,' he said. 'There's a long way still to go. The population has shifted in the last two years, and that means we have to pivot. Victims create victims: that's the tragedy. Recidivism is understandable. If you haven't been able to effect the change in yourself, and you're going back to an abusive partner, a pimp, a drug habit, it's catastrophic. The only success we have is when we never see anybody again. Returning customers aren't our raison d'être.'

We asked what good really looked like. 'We are very much judged on outcomes, curriculum outcomes,' he said, 'but we're pushing towards softer distance travel pieces as well. So – well done, you've just got two Level 2s in catering and hospitality and barbering; you've got your Level 2 in English and maths. Where are you going? Does that build your capacity? Does that empower you to think, yes, I can do this? Or have you just done it because it was there to be done?' He described it as the next stage of evolution – that journey, as he put it, from good to great.

He left us with a pithy quote that put prison employment nicely. 'You can choose to work at a prison,' he said. 'But the prison decides whether you stay or not.'

There are no women's prisons in Wales. Women

from Welsh courts are sent to prisons in England, a geographical and administrative reality that has drawn consistent criticism from penal reform campaigners and the Welsh government alike. The closest prison to which a woman from North or West Wales might be sent can be several hours away. Family contact, already difficult in any imprisonment, becomes harder to sustain. Children lose regular access to their mothers. Release planning is complicated by the need to engage services across a border the criminal justice system does not otherwise recognise.

Inside the prison, healthcare is the responsibility of NHS England. On the day a woman is released and crosses back into Wales, responsibility reverts to Welsh health services. The join between the two systems has been acknowledged by both governments as requiring significant improvement. Women who have established relationships with services inside the prison may find that continuity breaks precisely on the day they most need it.

The Welsh government has repeatedly called for a women's facility within Wales. None has materialised.

CHAPTER 8

Officer Training

'We weren't trained specifically to work with female
offenders. It was non-existent.'
BEV BUTLER

The question of how prison officers are prepared for work in the women's estate has been raised repeatedly by those who have spent careers within it.

The national training college for prison officers in England and Wales is at Newbold Revel in Warwickshire. The course runs for several weeks and covers restraint techniques, legal frameworks, suicide awareness, conflict resolution and the basics of wing management. It also covers, in theory, how to maintain appropriate boundaries with prisoners. What it does not and arguably cannot cover is the specific texture of how manipulation works in practice, how incremental it is, how each individual step feels defensible in the moment. The training describes the destination. It does not adequately prepare new officers for the journey, which is made up of very small decisions over a long period of time, each of which feels like nothing.

There is certain information a prisoner should never have about an officer: home address, car registration, financial situation, relationship status, family members' names. The training makes clear that sharing this is a disciplinary matter. What it cannot fully convey is how little any individual disclosure can feel like disclosure at the time. 'You look tired today.' 'You have been up all night with a cold.' You accept a packet of throat sweets. None of those steps feel like violations. Yet cumulatively, they are the mechanism by which an officer becomes compromised. The grooming of prison staff follows almost the same incremental logic as the grooming of vulnerable people outside. This is not a coincidence.

The high security estate has a significant problem with retaining female officers, too.

Bev Butler was among the first officers posted to New Hall when it made the transition to a women's prison and she described the training she had received with characteristic directness. It was aimed at the male estate, she said. How to control a riot, how to manage a violent inmate – the specific needs of women, the differences between male and female offenders, simply never came up. 'No. No, no, not at all,' she told us. 'When the training was, it was more aimed at the male estate, you know. More basic than that, you know, how to control the riot or, you know, a violent inmate, things like that, so no, it never really got talked about. So you weren't trained specifically to work with female offenders and the needs of women or the differences between men and women or all that kind of thing. Once it was non-existent, but it was a little bit of an eye-opener when we got to the prison, because we hadn't been told about it. A lot of it was on the male estate, because when we had our induction section, we didn't have a female governor or principal officer with us. It was all male. So it was only what they knew, really.'

Even the uniform of those early years spoke of a different world. When we asked Bev about it, she smiled. 'Yeah, it was blue. It was a soft hat. And if it was white or light blue? Bit more military-looking. Blue skirts, yeah. Yeah. We had to wear skirts. Oh, comfortable, really. It was all right. Not bad, but you didn't have to wear your hats inside the prison.'

Nicola Webster came to New Hall from a different background entirely, having served in the military before training as a nurse and moving into the Prison Service. Her account of her own induction illustrates how individual life experience could compensate for what formal training did not provide. 'You do an induction course, so you start to learn about prison life, the dos and the don'ts,' she told us. 'Being ex-military and being used to being given an order, I would follow that order. Being a bit older, I was a bit wiser, because a lot of staff that come into the Prison Service are very young and inexperienced. For me, I'd been in the forces, I'd been married, I'd got life experiences as a child as well. So I came with a different skill set and mindset, but I still listened to the officers that told us not to be groomed, not to bring stuff in, and all the basic stuff that is the foundation for working safely in that environment.'

The culture she encountered when she arrived was not always welcoming. 'Yeah, there's always going to be staff that, you know, I don't know how to say it, but some of them are difficult,' she said. 'I was bullied a little bit, but I got over it, and obviously moved up the ranks and ended up being a matron in the prison, so I didn't do badly. From the officer side, most of the staff are pretty supportive, and you know, we've all got to work together and keep safe, because there are some quite strong characters, prison wise, and the crimes that they committed have escalated dramatically over the years.

'The interest in the job has waned because at the end of the day, they're just waiting now for the pension, because the satisfaction in the job is not there,' she told us. 'The training of the officers, apparently, is abysmal. You know, the turnover of staff is terrible. So training and retention is probably at its worst. You've obviously got corruption as well, like the police service.' She was careful to add: 'I never physically saw it now, right. I've heard of it, but I haven't physically seen it now.' In some ways, she said, she missed the camaraderie and the support and the little bit that hopefully she had helped some of the women who came through the system. 'But I think my empathy just, it was tested to the limit, and you can only do that sort of job and give so much for so long, you know.'

Simon Peters did not enter the Prison Service through the conventional route. He had left school at 16, worked in a video shop and a pub, and then, standing in a Jobcentre staring at the board, thinking his life was going nowhere fast, spotted a card for the Prisoner Escort Service. 'I thought it sounded interesting if not a little kinky,' he told us. 'That was my entire career planning process.'

What followed gave him something that no training course could replicate. 'Inside vans that looked like budget versions of *Con Air*, moving prisoners across the country and learning more about people in three months than most people learn in 30 years,' he wrote. 'In that time I visited every prison in England and Wales. I dealt with men and women who were angry, terrified, funny, resigned, broken, dangerous and everything in between. I performed CPR on a man at Clacket Lane Services who died under my hands. That moment hit me hard. I had never seen death that close and suddenly I had the weight of someone else's final minutes on my chest. It set the tone for the years ahead. Things get real quickly in this work.'

When Simon joined the Prison Service in 1999, he was sent to Feltham. 'If you want to know what Feltham feels like, imagine a school that went badly wrong and then got worse,' he told us. 'First week you learn that alarms make your heart thump. Second week you learn not to show it. Third week you realise the only thing keeping the place standing are the staff and a lot of luck.'

What happened at Feltham in the years before he moved to Holloway was the event that changed how he understood the work. Zahid Mubarek was 19 years old, serving a 90-day sentence for petty theft. He was fatally attacked in his cell in the early hours of 21 March 2000, hours before he was due to be released, by his cellmate, Robert Stewart, a violent racist.

Simon had known Mubarek personally. 'Lovely, absolutely lovely boy,' he told us. 'That was another kind of catalyst for me of just like, you know – I knew all the people involved on the staff side. I knew him, and I knew the nuance, and I knew the context of how it came to pass, and I understood the pressures of the population, and I understood the accommodation pressures. And I also knew that when you'd been there for a 12-hour, 14-hour shift, when this is the last action of your evening, they just went, oh, we'll just put them in there, you know? And it was just mostly for their convenience, rather than having to shift other prisoners around at such a late hour and disrupt multiple people. And unfortunately, what happened happened, and it was a tragedy. But it was one of those moments where it really brings it home to you – yes, it's a job, but it's so impactful, and it's so direct, and it has such huge ripple effects. One action that you do can haunt you for the rest of your time. It was more carelessness at the end of a long shift and then people being hung out to dry. We didn't have cell-sharing risk assessments at that time. And when you've got one space left, and this person – I mean, Robert Stewart had a swastika tattooed on his head. And the consequence of the disruption that moving him would potentially cause – of course they decided, oh, we're just gonna stick them in there. And they never thought anything would happen.

And that's when things happen, and they're really bad, and then they haunt you.'

Simon articulated what underpins effective prison work in terms that had almost nothing to do with formal training. It came down, he said, to one thing: keeping your word. 'My word meant everything to me,' he told us. 'And one thing you never do is promise something unless you can deliver it. I do not mean you roll over and give people everything they ask for. But if you say you are going to do something, you do it. Because if you do not, you are never going to get anywhere with them. Trust works in a really odd way in prison. These people rely on you for everything. To eat, for medication, for visits, for everything. Everything that goes wrong in that environment is on you. If you can satisfy their legitimate needs within appropriate boundaries, you can start to make progress with them.'

The reputation that followed from that consistency was itself a resource. 'Because I knew everyone and knew how the prison worked, I could achieve things that other people seemed to struggle to achieve,' he said. 'It would often be as simple as going to whoever needed asking and saying, can we do this, or help me to do this. Through that kind of relationship you could achieve almost whatever you needed. Prison is all about no, no, no, you cannot. When you start saying yes, legitimately, things change.'

Twenty years of that work had left its marks. 'In 20 years I never fell foul of the disciplinary process, although I was involved in plenty of things,' he said. 'I once broke a prisoner's arm during a restraint. It was during a set of nights and he had smashed his cell to pieces, and I think he had taken something that made him go crazy. We went in and tried to de-escalate and he was having none of it. He ended up attacking us and during the restraint his arm snapped in an unusual place, between elbow and shoulder rather than the wrist or forearm. He did it, not me, by refusing to stop resisting. My stature meant I was very capable at violence, but it was never my go-to approach, ever. I would always be the one saying, let us go back and talk, let us reason, let us understand and see what we can do. But when it came to it, I had the aptitude for the techniques and I was good at that aspect of it.'

He was honest about the physical toll the work took. 'I found almost everything rewarding,' he said. 'Every day that was not running to alarm bells or cutting women down or taking people to hospital was a good day. Because that is what you want. You do good, and then you go home without bleeding. The amount of times I would phone my wife and say I am in casualty again. The amount of clothing I went through, ripped. I have one good knee and one completely busted one. The floors in those places are concrete. Every time I went down, I went down on the same knee. I have scars on my thumbs and fingers from glass, I was kicked in the leg by a violent young offender during a restraint and it opened down to the bone. I knew it was serious when I got up off the floor and took a step and my boot squelched as I walked forward. It was full of blood from my leg wound. I've had my thumb broken by a triad gang who turned on one of their own who changed his story and was giving evidence against them. On unlock for court they attacked him and were kicking him in the head. I intervened and was throwing them off him one by one. It was early in the morning and there were only a few staff around. By the time it was all over and we had restored order I knew something was really wrong with my thumb as it was painful and swollen. It's still not right, even now I can predict when it's going to rain,' Simon joked.

His final reflection on the work was perhaps the clearest statement of what distinguished the officers who lasted from those who did not. 'One thing this work has taught me is that you can never allow what a person in front of you has done to cloud your judgement or inform how you treat them,' he said. 'You need to know what they did and what they are capable of, for security and risk reasons. But you cannot allow it to dictate your humanity towards them. Because if you do, you are as bad as anyone else. I was not there when they did whatever they did, so I cannot judge them for it. I do not know what happened. What I do know is that they have gone through the process, they have gone through the system, and now they are here and I am here. In whatever capacity, we have to work together, because I have a job to do and they have a sentence to serve. I can be as decent as you like all day long, or we can butt heads. That is their choice.'

Suzy, whose 38 years in the Prison Service spanned roles from prison officer to governor, reflected on what the changing workforce had cost the system in terms of accumulated knowledge. She had noticed the difference sharply. 'I think it's quite transient now. Incredibly different,' she said. 'When I joined, the only person I knew in my first few years of service who left was a woman who got married and had children. Now people join for two years to get it on their CV, and they might want to be a psychologist or whatever afterwards. We had a spate of people joining who had no intention of doing it at all. They'd apply, go to Newbold Revel, which is residential for a few months, come back to the prison, walk on the landings, and decide it's not for them. But they'd just been paid and had accommodation for several months. No intention of actually staying. A waste of everyone's time and a place on the training that could have gone to somebody who meant it.'

The shift away from recruiting from the armed forces had, in her view, been a significant mistake. 'We used to go to the tri-service resettlement organisations and give talks on recruiting,' she told us. 'For people who were in their last year of being in the services, we used to go to presentations on the Prison Service as part of their resettlement. And then we were stopped doing that. And then I think there was a conscious decision, I'm pretty sure it was in the mid to late nineties, to not recruit ex-service people. And I think that was a mistake, because I think there's a real balance to be struck between the people who have all the psychology of it, and people who can run a good routine. You know, they can provide structure and boundaries and clear routines in a day, turn up, dress smart, be on time, and expect the prisoners to be the same. You need that institutional setting. It's discipline, but it's also boundaries.'

She had noticed the difference between those who were drawn to the work itself and those who saw it primarily as a step on a career ladder. 'You can always tell the people who like and feel more comfortable at front-line working with prisoners, and the people who are political animals doing it to say, I've got this on my CV, and I want to get to wherever,' she told us. 'You can spot them a mile off. This is a politician waiting. This is not somebody who's actually going to spend their career running a jail.'

Her own time at HMYOI Feltham as a principal officer had given her perspective on what the work demanded at the sharp end. 'It used to be called the Magic 922 – we were at 922 prisoners every night, always full,' she told us. 'We used to have about 120 beds out every day. You'd get there at six o'clock in the morning and discharge 120. Then from about mid-afternoon, 120 would come back in. Logistically, that's mind-blowing. My worst shift there – late nineties – from lunchtime on, I think we'd have four serious attempted suicides. We're cutting down people who are hanging. Walking towards a gate, walking past healthcare, there was another one. And that's what we were asking staff to do, day in day out. The resilience required, trying to save dead kids – or nearly dead kids. Most of them survived, but some of them didn't.'

The absence of support structures for those carrying that weight was something she returned to more than once. 'As a governor, you don't get any,' she told us. 'They did play with it occasionally – oh, you're going to have an hour with a psychotherapist once a month – and then they do it a couple or three times, and then the worst thing – you would never do this to your women as a psychologist treating them – but with the prison governor, they just suddenly randomly stopped without explanation, leaving you kind of hanging going, gosh, I've never heard from that psychotherapist again.'

On the question of institutional oversight, she was pointed. 'The Prison Service needs to get away from having one person doing the job and six people checking that they're doing it,' she told us. 'If you had six people doing the job and one person doing the scrutiny, you'd have a better service. I said this in my exit interview. When I joined, people joined, it was a job for life. But if you keep people two years now, you're doing well.'

What formal training could never adequately convey, Suzy described with one word: jailcraft. 'You can walk on to a wing and you could not identify what it is, but you will know that wing is bubbling,' she said. 'You just pick up a vibe, you feel uncomfortable; you couldn't say, oh it's because it's noisy or too quiet or whatever. You just pick it up and think, this wing is not in a good place. And actually a wing can be really noisy but in a really healthy way. You'll hear lots of chat and lots of laughter and screeching and running around, and you think, yes, this wing's fine, this is just how they are. And sometimes you walk on to a wing and think, this is noisy and this is not okay.

That jailcraft is missing with a lot of people now. Those subtle human behaviours.'

Not every officer arrived through the conventional route. Saj Zafar made history in 2001 when, at 24, she became the youngest Asian Muslim woman to be appointed as a prison governor in the United Kingdom – but her route there began much earlier, in a mining town in South Yorkshire where her family were among the first Asian households in the area.

'From being as young as seven, I knew that I was genuinely interested in psychology,' she told us. 'I was just interested in people. I remember the fascination that ignited it. My father and both of my parents were migrants, non-English-speaking people from Kashmir who arrived in the seventies, and of all the places in the UK, Dad got a job in a factory as a labourer in South Yorkshire, in a mining town. We were the first Asian families there, parachuted into this mining town. When I was young, we had a black and white TV. When Dad would come home, I would sit with him and he would turn on the TV and he would want to watch the news. He'd make me sit next to him and he'd say, what's the news? This was around the time of the Yorkshire Ripper. I remember when they caught him and I was just absolutely fascinated. I grew up watching all the thriller and crime programmes and I just knew that was the area I was going to go into.'

She went into forensic psychology and her first role placed her at the centre of a groundbreaking piece of work. 'This was 1996,' she told us. 'There were some very famous cases in the headlines at the time involving young people committing sexual offences, and as a knee-jerk reaction there was this discussion around funding, around whether rather than locking these boys away and forgetting about them, we needed to do something. The Americans were running the Sex Offender Treatment Programme and we had nothing of its nature here. So the government got some funding together, and when the boys in question were sentenced, they commissioned a therapeutic unit within the prison. It had never been heard of, never been done before. And I got the job. I got the job purely because I had done my degree thesis looking at young sex offending, so I was theoretically well versed.'

The work was dark and demanding, and the institutional environment was not always receptive. 'The governing governor was very much of the view that this had been imposed on him and he was worried about the safety of his staff,' she recalled. 'And then, of course, there is the hierarchy in prisons. If you're a robber, you sit above a burglar. If you're a burglar, you sit above a rapist. If you're a rapist, you sit above a paedophile. There is a ranking system. So these young boys were right at the bottom of the pile. I was selected, and for five years I sat in a room with those young people. The unit grew to 30 and we delivered the programme. It was a very dark period in many ways, a very sad period. Looking back now as a young person, I was just dedicated, eating and breathing those five years.'

That work brought her to the attention of a senior governor, who put her forward for the fast track leadership programme. The graduation ceremony and what came immediately after it was a moment she described with a precision that suggested she had turned it over many times since. 'At the graduation, it's a very grand affair. The band is playing, everyone is in smart uniform, the Home Secretary comes, you do the handshake, you have your picture taken and you are handed a brown envelope containing your first posting,' she told us. 'The understanding is that everyone is allocated a low-risk Category C prison, specifically chosen to give you 12 to 18 months to embed your learning and get your feet under the table. Nineteen people ahead of me picked up their envelopes. Category C working prisons. Some got Category D, an open prison. Then I opened my envelope and it said HMP Wormwood Scrubs. I actually thought it was a prank. I was quite used to people winding me up as I was the youngest. And then it became clear that it was not a prank. That is your jail. Category B, one of the most notorious prisons in Europe, and they were handing it to me as my starting posting.'

Her arrival at Wormwood Scrubs set the tone for much of what followed. 'There was a little bit of a media fanfare around the fact that a young Asian female was now a prison governor, because never in British history had that been accomplished before,' she said. 'So I became, I say this as a joke, the poster girl for the Prison Service's diversity agenda. Interestingly enough, I couldn't get into the prison on my first day. I turned up with my brown envelope and the officer at the gate didn't bother looking up. He just pointed and said, "no wives, girlfriends, sisters, probation officers, social workers, solicitors, it's the other door." I stood there trying to get his attention, and eventually I said, "no, I'll be working here, I'm your new governor." And it was: "Oh. Right. Okay."'

The institutional resistance was persistent. 'I spent a lot of time after that first posting trying to be accepted, trying to be respected as a leader,' she said. 'Because if you don't get the following, there is no leadership. People kept saying: this is not a white man in a suit of a certain age and maturity, ex-army or police. This person in front of us is something we are not accustomed to.'

Her response was to adapt, deliberately and at some personal cost. 'So I self-edited,' she told us. 'I was smart enough to know that I would not survive as a young Asian female unless I adapted. When I first arrived at Feltham as a psychologist, the governor there said to me: "you have got to appreciate that we have boys locked up here who are very close to your age. They will see a woman before they see anything else, and if I were you, you are going to have to learn there is a way of being in this jail if you are going to survive." And do you know what, I kept the receipt. I went straight back to Topshop. I got trousers, roll-neck jumpers. I took my contact lenses out and put my glasses on. I scraped my hair back, removed all make-up and jewellery, never wore heels. And that became my look, because it meant that people were not distracted by me. I call it defeminising myself. I had an alter ego, an armoured version of who I was, and everything I did was very controlled.'

The psychological cost of that sustained self-suppression extended well beyond the prison walls. 'My professional boundaries were not normal professional boundaries for someone in their early twenties,' Saj told us. 'They were very thick walls. My default starting position was distrust. If someone came to talk to me I would think: why are you talking to me? What information do you want? And it saddens me that some of those people were genuinely just being friendly. One of my girlfriends used to say: "Saj, your home is so clinical. Why do you not open the blinds?" I had recreated a kind of prison environment at home without even knowing it. No light, very sanitised, very routine. When I would walk through the front door, the first thing I would do was lock it and go straight to the bathroom for a shower, then eat, watch TV, go to bed. Very structured.'

Yet the same qualities that made institutional life so costly also made her effective inside it. 'In terms of managing prisoners, I was instinctively drawn to using my femininity to de-escalate,' she said. 'And I discovered that when I approached an incident with very little overthinking, going in as myself, I got results faster. I got compliance faster. And I think ultimately that led staff to think: actually, her methodology works. It elevates respect.'

One incident she recalled illustrated this. A prisoner had barricaded himself in, the water pipe was broken, blood was everywhere, and 1,500 men were locked up and getting hungry. Staff had been managing it for two and a half hours. 'So I got up and I marched to the scene, which is absolutely not what a Gold Commander is supposed to do,' she recalled. 'The staff were lined up at the door in full kit. I said, stand back. They stood back. I said to two officers: open the door. The door swung open and there was this prisoner, blood everywhere, cutting himself, and instead of ten officers with restraints, he had me standing in the doorway. I raised my hand and I said: "I need you to calm down and listen. What is the issue? What is it that you want?" And in the midst of all that chaos and blood and smeared walls, do you know what it was? He wanted to phone his mum. He had been transferred to a new prison without being able to let her know where he was going. I said: "is that what this is?" And he said yes. I said: "okay, we will sort that. Now you are going to stand down, we are going to close the door, you are going to stay where you are, and in one hour I will be back. Is that good?" And he said yes.'

At another secure environment, she encountered a prisoner whose self-harm she had managed to stop through a simple, repeated act of presence. 'We had a young prisoner serving a long sentence who was a serial self-harmer,' she told us. 'Every evening, without fail, this kid was just cutting himself. And my colleagues noticed that he never cut up on my watch. They said: "what the hell is going on?" I said: "do you want to know the truth? The last thing I do before I clock off is go to his cell. And

I said to him: tonight I am on duty and I do not want a call to say you have cut up tonight. When I get home I have two babies under the age of two, I have driven 17 miles, I do not want to drive back. I need you to make sure that tonight you do not do anything of that kind." And he looked at me and said: "okay." And he never did. Because his self-harming was attention-seeking. He could not cope with being confined in a cell, he needed to know that someone saw him.'

Then came the night in the segregation unit that changed things for the whole service. 'I find myself running to the segregation unit,' she said. 'When I reached there, I find that there are no staff, which is shocking, because it is always manned. I notice there's an alarm light flashing, so I know that the incident is on the top landing. I run up. The door is wide open, and there is a prisoner hanging with a noose around his neck – salivating, frothing at the mouth. The officer was holding him up by his knees, trying to prevent him – and he himself was red in the face. And as soon as I'd reached there, he looked over and he said, "ma'am, I can't hold him up any longer."

'Instinctively, I know – if his knees buckle, we will lose the prisoner. I run downstairs. There are no staff. I try to open up the desk, I grab the keys, and I go straight into the kitchen, and I unlock the knife cupboard. I take a knife out, I relock it, I go back upstairs, I jump on the bed and I cut the rope. The prisoner falls. The officer falls to the ground. By then, healthcare staff have arrived. They resuscitate him. He lives.'

The investigation that followed began the next morning. 'They asked me why I had done what I did,' she recalled. 'I said: "the only thing running through my mind was to save the prisoner. If I had let that officer's knees buckle and the prisoner had died, that officer would have spent the rest of his life with that." And when I went for the interview, the hearing, I said: "no amount of training ever prepares you for the incident in front of you. When your brain is triggered, rational logic can escape. You are dealing with instinct, and everything your training has put into you comes to the forefront at once."' She was not dismissed. A letter was placed on her HR file. And as a silver lining, the service issued small sheathed knives to every member of staff – worn on the belt with the keys, so that if there is a hanging, it can be cut quickly. 'That came from my incident,' she said.

Training provides the framework within which officers enter the work. The work itself is different: daily, cumulative, and understood not by what any course teaches but by learning the hard way.

CHAPTER 9

Entering Prison

'I can hear all the shouting. "Yo, new gal." From everywhere, "where you from?" And I thought, oh God, I just wanted to curl up in a ball and hope no one could see me.'
NEAH TUOHY

For most women, the journey to a custodial establishment begins in the back of a prison transport vehicle or 'sweatbox' as the prisoners call them. Simon had spent two years in the Prisoner Escort Service before he ever set foot in a prison as an officer, and his account of those journeys illuminates something about what it means to be in transit between one life and another.

'I had all of this paperwork and stuff in the back of the vans – everything that you could think about, where they've been to court, evidence produced, because prisoners have to have all of that in their possession to represent themselves and mount defences,' he told us. 'And then you would have the person behind a little door and you'd go and say, "hello, you all right? Do you want a sandwich?" That's so weird. And that enabled me to speak to some of these people, some of them at length, because some of these journeys were three hours.'

Reception is the first room inside the gate.

Bev had worked in reception at New Hall, and she described the routine search that preceded everything else. 'We always looked in the mouths, you know – open your mouth,' she told us. 'And I said, "what have you got in your mouth? Nothing. You've got something in your mouth. Come on, pass it over." It was a razor blade in her cheek. She'd lodged it in the pouch, like a pouch with her cheek. So she could self-harm with it. So we had a lot of mental health women, you know, that cut themselves and have had proper troubled lives. The police hadn't noticed this razor blade. And then she told the nurse that she had one somewhere else as well. The nurse said, "well, I'm not going up there." I said, "she's going to have to pass it." I think she did, eventually. Oh, dear. Some right ones.'

Bev described the range of women who came through reception at New Hall in its early years with the kindly equanimity of someone who had seen too much to be easily surprised. 'It could be anything,' she told us. 'One came in and she said there was a late library ticket or something – knocked up a few fines, and instead of paying the fines they just decided to take jail. She said "I don't know who is going to look after my dog." They could come in with a day or a week or whatever. And then, because we brought them in from Crown Court, they could have been longer sentences. Sometimes you'd bring in lifers. But on the main – drugs, dealing with drugs, or shoplifting, robbing, burgling, stuff like that.'

Eleanor Brown's arrival at New Hall on her first sentence was an experience she described with the precision of someone who had replayed it many times.

'And then I arrived at court and my barrister said, "right, we're looking at 18 weeks starting point, and I think he's going to push it up because you pissed him off,"' she said. 'So, coming up to the sentencing guidelines and how they categorise my offence, starting point only 26 weeks. If it's the statutory imposed 26 weeks, they're only gonna bring it down. So I thought I'd been looking at maybe 13 weeks. Do half of that, whatever, I can do it.' The judge said three years. 'And I remember going – the security guy just gets the paperwork and then takes you down to the cells. And I just remember, I sat with my head in my hands and I thought, that's what happened.'

The journey to the prison and the first moments in reception she described as a kind of suspended state. 'When I got there, I was the only person on the bus,' she told us. 'So it was only me that turned up, and it was so nice. I couldn't believe why I was there, whatever. The officer said to me, "can I get you a hot drink?" And I said, "a cup of coffee." And she was like, "just go and sit down." And that's when it hit me first – just the simple thing of that.'

The first night in the first night centre was manageable. The move to the main wing was not. 'I remember walking on to F Wing,' she said. 'You've gone from a clean cell to exactly what you'd imagine a prison cell to be. Metal bed with a blue mattress. Holes in all the walls with toothpaste and tissue rolls stuffed into them. The windows had sanitary pads and kids' socks shoved into the gaps around the bars. Red flooring. Graffiti all over the walls. The same space as the first night centre but now for two people. And then the first time they opened my door for association. No one's coming to get me. Okay. And I do remember that being a daunting feeling. Do I step outside, do I turn left, do I turn right? I do remember that being daunting.'

Neah Tuohy's first arrival at a women's prison at the age of 18 was an experience she described with laughter and a kind of retrospective disbelief. She had been going to prison on her birthday. She had just fake-tanned herself for the birthday plans she would no longer be keeping.

'I was gonna wash it off the next day, like you leave it on,' she told us. 'So when I got to go to prison the next morning, I haven't washed it off, and it goes really, really orange if you don't wash it off. So then I'm there looking like this little – and I thought, oh, my God, I wish I had a tracksuit. I was pouring out of a pair of trousers or something.' She was laughing. 'Oh no, honestly. I'm only 18. I can hear all the shouting. "Yo, new gal." From everywhere, "where you from?" And I thought, oh God, I just wanted to curl up in a ball and hope no one could see me. But it was like, that's not gonna happen, and now it's gonna get even worse, 'cause you have an idea you're looking more vulnerable and you stick out, so you're the very youngest – the youngest, by definition, in the country that day.'

She had known, she told us, that she was going to be tested the moment she walked on. She had prepared herself. 'So they're all following me, a load of girls. I know they're gonna come. They're gonna try and rob me. I know they are. Whatever happens that day is all in my way.' So she had stood her ground. 'My heart palpitations – I've gone white, gone white.' She had stood off and told them what was what. They had all come up to her saying they respected her for it, that they had only been joking. 'You fucking idiots,' she told them. 'So I never had any trouble again. You had to put yourself in those situations. Yeah.'

For those who entered the system as children, the experience of first custody was shaped differently, by institutions designed to occupy a space between school and prison without fully resembling either. Anastasia arrived at Rainsbrook Secure Training Centre at the age of 16, having been convicted of robbery at Snaresbrook Crown Court and sentenced to 33 months. She had never expected to be sent there.

'I never thought I'd be sent to prison as my parents were a working-class family,' she told us. 'My father a plumber and my mother a police officer, but I was easily led and influenced at that age.' The transport was not a prison van in the conventional sense. 'It was a little van with blacked-out windows,' she said, 'and they give you, like, a sandwich, some crisps, and a drink on the way there, but obviously I didn't want to eat because I was just in shock.'

When you get there, she told us, you go through the doctors, and as you walk out it's all in a circle, more like flats, with a park in the middle. 'As I got on to the unit, I didn't get to see anyone at this point because I got there quite late, so everyone was already locked in,' she said. 'As you walk on to the unit, you've got, like, two side doors, you've got, like, a dining room area, a living room area and a kitchen area, and we're allowed to use all of those areas up till nine o'clock at night until obviously we get locked in. And there's another three cells, and then there's, like, an office.'

She started on Burliston unit, which held around five girls. Because she was older, she was moved to Kilsby unit, where she met Lorraine Thorpe. 'When I was let out,' she told us, 'there was a girl actually there that I knew from Moulton. So, obviously, I was a bit less nervous then, if you know what I mean.'

The regime at Rainsbrook was structured around four behaviour levels – Bronze, Silver, Gold and Platinum – with Platinum bringing an extra hour of association in the evenings. On weekends, the units could visit each other for an hour each, though not each other's rooms. Education ran in the mornings and afternoons. The cells had no windows that could be opened, she told us – hard plastic only, because the young people were self-harming. Everything was designed around what could not be done, as much as what could.

The education, she found, was pitched far below her level. 'I was a Level 2 student and I was doing Entry Level 3 work, with questions like which one is the tallest tree, as questions which really insulted my intelligence,' she said. She was there for seven months, long enough to know Lorraine Thorpe well, before an incident on the enhanced unit led to her being moved to Eastwood Park's 17-year-olds' wing the following day. 'I actually hit one girl around the head with a draining board holder in the kitchen,' she told us matter-of-factly. 'And I was then shipped out the next day to HMP Eastwood Park juvenile wing for all 17-year-old girls.'

The juvenile wing at Eastwood Park was, in her assessment, the worst placement of her sentence. 'There's about 12 girls,' she told us. 'But yeah, it was just 17-year-olds on that one. There were more stuck together. We couldn't really get out of there or mix with anybody. And there's only 12 of us. We used to argue quite a lot, as you can imagine. We used to live upstairs and then we used to go to education downstairs. So this was where we felt like we were just stuck in the same building constantly, apart from if we were allowed outside. And that was just contained for all of us.'

On her 18th birthday, she was moved across to the adult wing. 'The first person I saw, she was like this little slight one with a hunchback, and she was like, I don't know, I've never seen anyone look like that alive, but looking like something out of a horror film, and I started crying to the juvenile staff, and I was like, don't leave me here,' she told us. 'And then I went into the cell, and literally, the toilet was at the end of my bed, and there were ants coming out of the safe. Oh, I'd never been in such – like, it was just disgusting, to be honest. And I'd say it took something, because everyone was on about drugs, everyone kept knocking on your door for dog ends and stuff like that.'

The experience of arriving at each new prison carries its own vibe. There is the reception desk, the officer going through the paperwork, and sometimes – in prisons that use prisoner labour in that role – another inmate behind the counter, cheerful and seemingly ordinary.

Anastasia described arriving at Drake Hall after a transfer from New Hall. The woman who greeted her at reception, she told us, came across as really nice. 'She seemed nice, like having a bit of a speak with her,' she said. 'And then it's not until obviously you get on to the induction house, people were saying, "Don't get speaking to that girl." She was a high-profile co-accused in a serious child sexual abuse case. And I did end up with her, when I came off the induction house; I ended up two doors down from her on Bristol House. And she stayed in her cell, but there was this one girl that used to visit her, and they used to, like, chill together.'

Dainya arrived at Bronzefield first, on remand, and then was moved to Holloway. Her account of the first weeks focuses less on the logistics of arrival than on the immediate social landscape she walked into.

'At the start, I was lucky,' she told us. 'Three of the girls in my dorm were people I had already met in Bronzefield while on remand. That familiarity made a difference straight away. There was already a level of trust, a level of understanding. We naturally fell into a rhythm together –

keeping the space clean, respecting each other's boundaries, looking out for one another. Over time, we became like sisters.'

The dorm itself – five beds, one toilet, no privacy – had the potential to be really grim. 'One of the biggest issues for me was hygiene,' she told us. 'The four of us had a standard. We liked things clean, organised and respectful, especially because we were sharing such a small space. Then you'd get someone come in who was the complete opposite. And that toilet was grim. Proper grim. There were times you'd go in there and just stand still for a second, debating whether you even wanted to use it. And then there were silverfish. Tiny, grey insects, moving fast across the floor. I had never seen anything like that before in my life. Little things like that build up. People think it's just prison, you get on with it – but when you're living it every day, those details matter.'

For women who move through multiple establishments – and most do, particularly those serving longer sentences – the experience of first arrival repeats itself, each time with its own variation. The shock diminishes; the vigilance required does not.

Neah passed through eight women's establishments over the course of a decade. She described what you learn to read in the first hours at each new place. 'The atmosphere on the wing was always eerie, like unpredictable,' she told us. 'You never know what's going to happen from one minute to the next. Really unsettling. There was quite a bit of violence, but a lot of it behind closed doors.

It was more the fear of violence. You don't know who's standing behind you in the queue. You don't know who's going to lose it. Something settling, yes, but in the end you get more used to the unpredictability and you learn to adapt to it. You develop a radar. You can walk on to a wing and feel that something isn't right without hearing or seeing anything. You just feel that something's about to kick off.'

Anastasia described the ritual of arrival by bus at an unfamiliar prison, and what waited at the gate. 'When you pull up on the bus, you have all of the lesbians waiting to see who's going to get off the bus,' she told us. 'They'll get the newcomers. I had a horrendous first two or three weeks.' The social dynamics of a new wing were established within hours, and a woman's position within them could be set in a single encounter. The art of the first days was staying visible enough not to be targeted, and inconspicuous enough not to become a focus.

The first days in custody establish the conditions of everything that follows: what work is available, which wing you are on, who your cellmate is, where your place in the pecking order will be.

CHAPTER 10

Daily Life in Prison

*'Six minutes to my mum was about 40p. Six minutes.
If you told me I could sit behind that door for ten hours
but have unlimited calls, I'd have been all right. But to
know the phone is there and you can't afford it –
that's what finishes people off.'*
ELEANOR BROWN

The daily routine in a women's prison is built around a framework of work, education and adjudication that has changed in its particulars over the decades, but remains recognisable in its essentials. In the earlier years of New Hall as a women's prison, the range of activity was broader than it would later become. Bev recollected it to us with her typical fondness and warmth. 'They'd get jobs confirmed by an officer who would find them work,' she told us. 'At the time, we had a farm, so you'd have outside work as well. You'd have trusted inmates going out on the farm, feeding the pigs and things like that, getting the cows in. Then that got sold off eventually. And then there were gardens; they would go out as well sometimes. There was plenty of jobs going on, and then across in the education unit, so they could go up there and carry on studies or learn something new. There was always something going on.'

The disciplinary structure sat alongside the daily regime, and Bev described the adjudication process from the perspective of the officer responsible for managing it. 'That's where we did the adjudications as well for the governor, you know, when you put somebody on report,' she explained. 'You'd take them over to the segregation unit that morning, and then the governor would come across, do the adjudication, and either keep them there or send them back to the wings with a slap on the wrist.'

Work in prison occupies the hands and fills the hours, and in some cases provides the only structure a woman has ever had. Its content varies from the genuinely skilled to the numbingly repetitive, and those who have experienced both remember the difference clearly.

Dainya offered us a particularly striking and thoughtful account of what prison work meant to her:

Being in prison, a lot of us found ways to make the time go by. Most women either chose education – English, art, music, things like that – or they got a job. I tried education, but honestly, I found it boring. It just didn't hold me. I can't even remember everything they offered – it was a long time ago – but I knew pretty quickly it wasn't for me.

So I decided to work.

First, I tried being a gym orderly. It was all right for a little while, but I quickly realised it wasn't for me.

It didn't feel beneficial or interesting enough to keep me there. I needed something with more purpose, something that would actually make the time feel worthwhile.

That's when I applied for the kitchen.

The kitchen was one of the easier jobs to get, even with knife handling and all of that. What drew me to it was simple – I heard you might get the chance to cook your own food sometimes, and at least I'd be able to see how the food was made instead of just eating it without thinking. Most of the work was food prep – making sandwiches for the women around the prison, preparing desserts, washing up and cleaning. We didn't have to deliver the food; the 'trolley dollies' handled that part.

But again, after a while, I got bored.

That's when I really started to understand something about myself – I didn't want to be stuck inside all day. I needed space. I needed fresh air. I needed something that felt a bit closer to freedom, even though I wasn't free.

That's when I started hearing about the gardens.

People would say you're outside most of the day, working with plants, doing agriculture. Straight away, I thought, that's me. There was something bigger attached to it too. If you worked in the gardens and proved yourself, you could earn a red band. That meant more freedom – moving around the prison more independently – and with that came a different level of respect from officers.

That mattered to me.

Getting into the gardens wasn't easy. There were

limited spaces, and you had to be seen as a 'good prisoner'. I had to wait, especially after an incident where I ended up being escorted everywhere. I'd slapped a girl for making a stupid remark – something I didn't even need to involve myself in. Looking back, I could've handled it differently. I didn't need to react at all.

Because of that, I was put on an orange folder. It was for vulnerable prisoners or those in trouble, and it meant staff monitored you more closely and wrote reports on your behaviour. I hated it. It brought attention I didn't want, and in that environment being seen as vulnerable could make you a target.

Eventually, I got my chance in the gardens – but not without warnings. Everyone kept talking about one particular job run by a lifer everyone seemed scared of. I remember thinking, please don't let me be placed with her.

But that's exactly what happened.

A lifer. Tall, strong, a Rastafarian woman who didn't play games. She was direct, vocal and carried authority without trying. When I first saw her, I was intimidated straight away. I was 19, thinking, this woman is in here for killing someone – and I'm working with her.

But she became one of the most important people I met in prison.

She taught me everything – bins, recycling, how to work properly and at a steady pace. She noticed I was a fast learner. We started talking more, and I warmed to her. She warmed to me. At one point she said, 'You're the best one I've got.' That stayed with me.

We built respect.

To understand prison properly, you have to understand the system inside it.

A red band meant you were trusted. It allowed you to move around the prison without constant officer escort, apart from needing doors unlocked. It wasn't given freely – you had to earn it and be approved by the governor. It changed how you were seen and gave you a small sense of freedom and responsibility.

The gardens were one of the best jobs you could get. Working outside on the prison grounds gave you space from the pressure inside. It didn't erase where you were, but it made it easier to breathe.

Then there was the dorm – five women sharing one room, one sink, one toilet. No privacy. Just different personalities and energy constantly clashing. A single cell, on the other hand, was your own space. That became my goal.

A lot of my deepest thoughts came at night.

Lying on that uncomfortable bed, layering blankets just to make it bearable because the mattress dipped like a hammock. Never fully comfortable. Never quiet.

You'd hear everything.

Women shouting out of vented windows – 'window warriors'. Lovers talking from cell to cell. Banging on doors. People shouting through hatches, asking for medication or attention. There was always noise. Never a silent night.

And not to mention some of the male staff.

There were times their behaviour felt uncomfortable and inappropriate. In a women's prison that added another layer of tension. Personally, I didn't feel male staff always belonged in that environment, especially when boundaries didn't always feel clear or respected.

And in those moments, my mind would run.

I'd think, get me out of this concrete jungle. Some of the younger women – 18 to 21 – I saw as wild, not in judgement, but in how chaotic everything felt. It was survival, emotion, reaction, all happening at once.

Anastasia also told us about the full range of work she performed. At Eastwood Park, she spent five months in Workshop 5. 'You'd have a box of plastic gloves and literally you'd have to count the gloves out, and you'd have to put them into plastic bags, and then the officer would weigh them at the end,' she told us. 'I tried to cheat when I first got in there, and I just shoved in as many as I could, but she'd make me count them all out again. I ended up going crazy. I'm not one for that, so they put me into hairdressing in the end. I just couldn't cope with that. Imagine doing that eight hours a day.' The hair salon, when she reached it, was different. 'It actually felt like a workplace,' she said. 'I didn't feel like I was in jail for most of the day. If you know what I mean, apart from the dusting down of the scissors and that at the end.'

At New Hall, she sorted CDs – putting one CD in a box, the paper of the CD case in the box, the plastic cover in a box – before returning to hairdressing. At Drake Hall, it was waste management: walking to different houses, collecting bins. Each job carried a small wage, and the wage carried its own meanings. Women worked so they could put money on their phone account, so they could buy things from the canteen, so they could, in some cases, send money out to their children.

Dainya described what work meant in terms of access to basic things. 'I started in education, then moved into the kitchens, and later worked in the gardens,' she told us. 'The food on the wing was poor. Most of the time, I kept it simple – pastries, sausage rolls, noodles, cheese and onion pasties. Working in the kitchens changed everything. Suddenly, I had access to proper food. There was a Jamaican woman working there, and her food was on another level. Full of flavour, proper portions – it felt like real food, not just something to get you through the day. In a place where so much feels controlled and limited, something as simple as a good meal becomes comfort. It gives you a moment of normality.'

The gardens, she said, brought her into contact with longer-term prisoners in a different way from anywhere else in the prison. 'There was one woman in particular. Someone everyone else seemed to be wary of, even scared of. But with me, she was different. She took a shine to me, and we built a genuine relationship. She looked out for me. She would cook for me, check on me, and if I was unwell, she would send food up to the wing.' It showed her something important, she said. 'People aren't always what they seem.'

The social structure of the wing operates according to its own logic, and those new to it learn it quickly. Nicola Webster observed it with a clinical eye. 'There's a hierarchy on the wing, isn't there?' she said. 'You've got top dog. It's a bit like *Porridge* – some of those things do go on. There's a hierarchy, and it's just the way of life, isn't it? People cope and survive, I suppose. And for me, there are people that come into prison that are very green, but go out a lot wiser. You come in as a basic criminal and go out as an expert.'

Juli Flintoff described the dynamics and status around her cleaning team with a combination of exasperation and amusement. One woman ran the landing as if she were managing a small company. When a dispute arose one day – a used tampon left in a shower drain, and a cleaner who refused to pick it up – Juli resolved it in the simplest way she could find. 'I just went and got a pair of gloves, picked it up, put it in the bin where it should have been, and I said, "right, can we get back to work now?"' she told us. 'She just stared at me. And I said, "I will never ask you to do something that I won't do myself. But don't ever refuse again." And she never did. She saw respect.'

The privilege system – Basic, Standard and Enhanced – created its own social stratifications. Cath Thompson described how manipulation of that system began almost immediately on the wing. 'They try to sort of suck up to you,' she told us. '"How are you doing today, miss, having a good day?" "How are you feeling? Are you all right?" "I'm treating you well, yeah?" And then they'll turn around a couple of days later and say, "oh, can I have the paper first this week?" "No, it's not your turn." "Can I get my canteen earlier today?" "No, you get it." when you normally get it. So they're just trying to get those little privileges, get little things extra that the others don't get. But you can see them coming a mile off.'

Cath was the first female officer at Leeds to become pregnant on the landings, and the way prisoners responded to that personal change told her something about how the wing read its officers. 'They didn't know what to do with me,' she said. 'I said, look, "till I'm six months, can I go on the landings, and then go into the centre?" So they said yes. But then you get the consequence. "Can I have my VO brought forward?" "No, you don't get it until it's due." "Can I have my weekly early?" "No, you can't have it till next week, because it's not due till next week."'

The prisoners had read the change. The personal becoming visible, whether pregnancy, divorce, illness, or anything, registered immediately on the landing as a possible opening. 'An officer told me at Styal when I was training: "once you give them something, it's very hard to take it back." And it is.'

The difference between how men and women experience the daily texture of custody is something almost every contributor described in similar terms, regardless of whether they had known both estates.

Suzy had worked in both. 'The other thing I'd say is really different about women is that they still hold the responsibility of the family, even if they're inside,' she told us. 'They might have kids, and they'll be thinking all the time about, oh God, I hope they've done their homework. Have they got their school uniform? Are they doing what they need to do? Women are very much trying to run the home and manage the kids from inside. They all try to work so they can send money out so the kids can go on a school trip or whatever. And the men will be on the phone going, send me some money, I need some trainers.'

Simon drew a similarly sharp distinction. 'Women are more outward in terms of emotion,' he told us. 'They want to tell you what is happening. Men keep everything to themselves. The only thing men will tell you is what they are going to do. They shout and scream and say, "I am going to punch you in the face." And they will, because they have told you that is what they are going to do. Whereas women will not necessarily be as overt in their actions, but they will be with their emotion. They want you to understand where they are coming from.'

Cath, who had worked in both male and female establishments, offered a more domestic comparison. On hygiene, she was unequivocal. 'Women are far dirtier,' she told us. 'Women would rather go and sit in a cell and have a gossip. You'd think that they'd want it. But I used to literally walk round at New Hall shaking my head. I worked on Unit Two, and I'd shake my head. And you'd say, "well, you're a woman." I said, "yes, I'm a woman." I said, "but you're women." I said, "I wouldn't like to see your steady homes." Because honest to God, you shut the door, and dust used to fly across the floor – like tumbleweed. You know what you see in a cowboy film? That was it.' Men, she said, would clean out when asked and then shower. Women would find any reason to avoid it. 'On a night time, going round to lock up or do checks, I'd try and do the whole landing. So they'd get a clean-out at the weekend and a shower. But the women – they'd much rather just go and sit in a cell and have a gossip.'

Eleanor described how the prison economy worked in practice, and what it meant for maintaining contact with the outside world. 'You can have £1,000 of private money sitting in your account,' she told us. 'But you can only spend your weekly drop. If you're enhanced, you get £33. Standard is £21. Basic is £5. And if your private account is at zero, you get nothing unless you've been working – if you work, you get £3.80 a day, unemployed you get 50p. That weekly drop has got to cover your phone bill, your canteen, everything. The maximum you can build up in spends is £100. So you can be the richest person in jail and have ten grand in your account – completely pointless. You can't touch it.'

On the cost of maintaining contact with family outside, she was unambiguous. 'You've got a PIN number – a seven-digit code. You type in your mum's number, tap in your PIN, and if that number's registered on it, it'll connect. You can't ring anyone who isn't on there. Six minutes to my mum was about 40p. Six minutes,' she told us. 'If you told me I could sit behind that door for ten hours but have unlimited calls, I'd have been all right. But to know the phone is there and you can't afford it, or you're rationing your calls – that's what finishes people off. It doesn't matter who you are. It's really wrong.'

The introduction of in-cell phones across the estate transformed the daily emotional landscape in a way that Suzy described as a revelation. 'Having phones in the cells for women was just a revelation,' she told us. 'Because they want to be able to say goodnight to their kids every night. They want to be able to let them know Mum is still there. They still hold that responsibility very strongly. Having that phone – the ability to say goodnight, I love you, see you on Saturday – changes the quality of daily life completely.'

Yvonne Simpson remembered food booking with a kind of resigned disbelief. 'They wouldn't give you anything special unless you got it on canteen, so a week before you have to decide what you're going to crave next week,' she said. 'Just if you're lucky.'

The social landscape of the wing reflects the social landscape outside it, with layers of community, solidarity, pressure and exclusion that those unfamiliar with prison life might not expect. Neah described the groupings that formed on exercise at Holloway with the directness of someone who had navigated them carefully.

'You'd go out on the exercise and you'd have to fall in,' she told us. 'The Black girls got their own cliques, basically. That's where we were mainly. I used to just float through. 'Cause I just always kind of been like that, I would talk to everyone. But you're not – which is why – you know, you're not welcome if you're really welcome by a Black girl if you're white. Things like that. It's not about being like that, but there is, like, the Black community. A lot of the Black girls want to recreate – if you're a new girl and you're Black, you should be with us, and they will be made to feel like that. Like, you know, we're the minority, but nowadays in prison, they're not. The white people are the minority.' With Romanian women, she said, it was more language-based – a natural clustering rather than a pressured one. 'But with the Black girls, it's more of a pressure thing – like, you should stand together.'

The experience of daily life differs significantly between those serving long sentences and those passing through on short ones. The lifers know the place; the short-termers create the chaos. Suzy described the contrast from a governor's perspective.

'Your worst ones were the short-termers,' she told us. 'They were just like crazy kids, still in the way. Whereas the lifers just, you know, got their senses and settled into it. Because if you've got a female lifer – take Rose West – she wouldn't pose a threat to prison officers, I wouldn't have thought. She knows that her behaviour in here is going to determine what happens, isn't it? She's got to earn her way through the system as well. So to get to an open prison, they don't just look at the record. They'll be finding out – probation, psychologists, therapists, the parole board finally saying you can now go to the next prison. So they have to work for it. Strange, really, when you think of what they've done. But they've accepted they're in for a long time and they got their heads down. They're not fighting the system.'

And then there were the women who came back so regularly that the place had become genuinely home. Suzy returned to this more than once, and each time with the same quality of feeling – not quite despair, not quite acceptance, but something in between.

'Most of them come in time and again, time and again, time and again,' she told us. 'Actually, their prison becomes their home. Women come in and say, "is my room still available?" They talk about it like it's home. They say, "so-and-so – can I be with her?" And actually, the women living on the street – you release them, say on a Thursday, and they'd be going out the gate going, "bye, see you Monday." Because actually, they will tell you that being in a prison where the bed is clean and warm and dry and you get food, and if you've got an addiction within 24 hours you'll see a doctor – if you go out on the street, you're scrounging for food out of the bins at the back of Tesco, you're sleeping in the park, you're being raped most nights. And this is a reality. Don't think this just happens in Third World countries. This is the reality for many women. And if you go to your doctor and say, "I've been taking heroin, I've got a problem, I need help" – the doctor will say, "that's fine, I'll sign you up for services. There's about a three- to six-month waiting list." So they commit a crime to come to prison to access the services.'

Christmas comes. Birthdays come. Eid comes. The calendar does not stop.

CHAPTER 11

Special Occasions

'I had my 17th, 18th, 20th and 21st birthdays in prison. It is just a normal day. But some of the girls would wrap me presents in newspaper.'
ANASTASIA SEVERN

The calendar continues behind bars. What changes is everything that surrounds them: the rituals, the people, the freedom to do anything about what you feel. What remains is the feeling itself, unaltered and in many cases intensified by confinement to a degree that those on the outside rarely consider.

Christmas is the occasion that requires the most institutional effort and generates the most complicated emotional weather. In women's prisons it carries weight, because the women most likely to be inside at Christmas are also the women most likely to be separated from children who are spending the day elsewhere.

'Christmas is an odd time in prison because nobody wants to be there,' Suzy Dymond-White told us. 'The staff would rather be with their families and the prisoners would rather be at home with theirs. They kind of make the most of it. There's always a small element of the women who don't have a home or a family anyway, so they're quite into it. The staff go above and beyond. The chaplains do a wonderful job. But you've got to get the balance right, offering time for reflection because it is a very sad time, and also time to celebrate, which sometimes feels a little bit hollow because you're celebrating and you think, actually, maybe I shouldn't be celebrating as such. There's this slightly odd dynamic.'

From a governor's perspective, the institutional management of Christmas demands both effort and presence. 'Christmas is a really big deal in women's prisons,' Suzy told us. 'You spend quite a lot of time trying to make it work. The duty governor – who could be the governing governor – would go round on Christmas morning and wish everybody Happy Christmas. And you'd try and make it as special as possible. There would be little extras and little treats. They would be encouraged to decorate their cells, and they could make decorations, and have a Christmas tree on the wing. You'd get the Christmas dinner, which they all moan about, whatever it is. But it is a Christmas dinner. There would be a festive atmosphere if you could manage it.'

She had made a point of going in herself on Christmas Day throughout her career. 'As governor, I always went in on Christmas Day,' she told us. 'Went in in the morning, went to the multidenominational church service, always visited all the wings, judged the best-dressed wing competition, helped serve the Christmas meal, and then went home. I understand now that has fallen away and governors don't bother to go in on Christmas Day. If you were head of a big boarding school and you had children there over Christmas, you would be there for them. If you were running a hospital or a care home, the manager would go in and see everybody. I felt it was the duty of a governor. I don't think they do that now. It's really sad.' She had made clear why she felt it mattered. 'I think it matters.' We understood what she was saying. It costs you something to be there, and you should be willing to pay it. The women knew that. They noticed who turned up and who sent someone else.

The calendar of occasions extended well beyond Christmas. Suzy described a range of events that, precisely because they were small and low stakes, carried a significance inside that they would never have carried outside. 'It's not just Christmas,' she said. 'Other festivities: we try to put on a sports day in the summer to get people out and active. Minor games, they're called. Little kind of sporting competitions, teams of six, relay races, using a ball or some bollards. They get really involved. Women love a competition. It's a really good way to engage them. International Women's Day is always quite a big thing in women's prisons. Design a poster, write a poem, paint someone you find inspiring, write a bit of a biog. There might be a trivial little prize at the end, like a packet of biscuits or a lipstick. But that's actually really big; it's the pride of winning that's the thing.'

International Women's Day occupied a place in the women's estate calendar for a reason Suzy articulated precisely. 'It's a much bigger deal in a women's prison than anywhere else,' she told us. 'Because you're making a point, aren't you? These are women. This day is about women. And there would be events and activities laid on – external speakers, workshops, recognition of what the women had achieved. It was one of those days where you could feel the place shift a little. Like something that usually went unacknowledged was, just for a day, being acknowledged.'

The cooking competitions she described had a quality that went beyond competition. 'We used to have an annual cooking competition,' Suzy told us. 'Each wing would put in a submission, and then there would be a judging. We would try to have as many external judges come in. And the women were proud of that. They really were. It wasn't something done at them. It was something they did, and were judged on, and could win. That kind of thing matters enormously. You're not just a number in a cell, you're someone who makes a better Christmas cake than the woman on the next wing.'

The format could vary, and the spirit it produced did not. 'We used to do one where women could enter a sort of cook-off,' she said. 'We had a training kitchen, which was part of education. Women from different cultures and backgrounds would pick a member of staff to be their assistant, and I did it, so they'd say, can you chop those vegetables, can you wash that for me. The women were in charge. They'd cook something that was a memory for them, from their growing up, some sort of cultural history. Maybe from the Caribbean, they'd do jerk fish, or whatever they wanted to do. Then they'd present the dish to the whole group and talk about it. It was my grandmother's favourite cake. She taught me this, and this is my memory of growing up. And then everybody would share the food, try a bit of each dish. They used to love all that stuff. That proper engagement.' The marking of religious occasions had the same quality. 'And there's Eid,' she said. 'The catering department would put on a special meal and the chaplains, because they represent the full range of religions, would come together and sometimes have a bit of a party. I'd often go. I've had prisoners henna design my hands. They love sharing their culture. You invite other people in and then they learn about that culture, and I think that makes for a much richer environment.'

Yvonne's first night at Styal was the week before Christmas and despite hearing of the attempt at festivities, the reality was clearly very nuanced. Her account of trying to phone her children that night belongs to the earlier chapter. What it showed though was how completely the institution controls even the most basic human act.

Yvonne also described an argument about the in-cell phones that showed how easily a resource intended to help generated its own frictions. 'Of course it would, because there'll be people wanting it at certain times,' she said. 'Yeah, and especially if there's a hierarchy in the house, they'd want that phone for longer. And you're sitting there thinking, this is my kid's bedtime. Time's ticking away.

And there were of course horrendous arguments. So yeah, unnecessary, unnecessary.'

When a prison's Christmas is managed well, the small dignities – a phone call, a few minutes of privacy, a mince pie left outside a cell door – cost almost nothing and mean an enormous amount. When they are managed badly, the absence of those things amplifies everything else that is already lost.

The management of religious observance across a diverse prison population is both a legal requirement and a daily negotiation. Every prisoner's cell card carries a religion field. It is, in theory, a record of genuine belief. In practice, it is also a menu.

'The religion on the cell card is very important for a number of reasons, and not all of them are genuine,' Suzy told us. 'Being Jewish in a prison means you get Kosher food. And Kosher food in prison is a lot better. A lot better. So you get people who will convert to Judaism purely to get the Kosher food. You get people who will use Islam and Ramadan to get the additional night pack. Because the night pack is better than what they normally get. This is just human behaviour. If you put a better meal on the other side of a religious declaration, some people will make that declaration. You can't really blame them for it. But it does make the religion field somewhat approximate.'

Ramadan transformed the daily rhythm of the wing for those observing it and for those who were not. Eid, at the end of Ramadan, was an occasion in its own right.

'At Eid you'd get samosas,' Neah told us. 'Which is

better than your standard food. Yeah, I converted in prison. Not really converted. I would just do Ramadan in there, because you got better food. You got your Suhoor – your food before and food after. So I used to do Ramadan there to get the better food. But then I'd carry the spirit of it too. I ended up doing it genuinely as well. But I started it for the food. So many people do.'

The religious provision extended beyond the major faiths. 'There's religion,' Neah said. 'There's the mosque, the church, the Jehovah's Witnesses. I've never heard of a synagogue in a women's prison. I've known Jewish prisoners but no synagogue. The Muslims, if you're not Asian and you go along, they think you're coming for the food. Half the time I was. They have samosas and all that. But then you've got to get down on the rug and do all that and they go, you clearly don't know what you're doing. The different religions come with different perks. Ramadan, you fast for a month but at the end you get the big Eid party. So it's like, do you want to fast for a month but eat better than you have in years at the end? Surprisingly popular.'

The Jehovah's Witnesses attended the prison weekly, Neah said, with persistence. 'They used to come in once a week and you'd do a year's study with them. Some girls really genuinely got into it. They were very persistent. Every single week without fail: do you want to study with us? And some of the women, it really did give them something. Something to structure their thinking around. Something outside themselves.' She reflected on it. 'Religion in prison is interesting. People who've never given it a thought on the outside suddenly find it. When everything else is stripped away, some people reach for something bigger than where they are.'

Visits occupy a category of their own in the special occasions landscape of the prison year. They are not annual or seasonal but they carry, each time, the full emotional weight of the relationship that produced them.

Dainya described what a visit looked like from the wing. 'One of the hardest things to witness was visits,' she told us. 'Watching the mums spend time with their children – holding them, playing with them, trying to be present in that small window of time – and then having to say goodbye. You'd see them holding it together during the visit, putting on a brave face. But when they came back on to the wing, that's when it hit them. The crying, the silence, the emptiness after. There's a particular quality to that grief. It is completely ordinary and completely unbearable at the same time.'

Every time someone comes back from a visit, Suzy told us, they are searched. That is a fixed point. Because visits are the primary route for contraband into the prison. The women know this. The searches are thorough. 'And this means that a woman who has just spent an hour with her children comes back in and is strip-searched before she can go back to her cell,' she said. 'The emotional whiplash of that – from the visit to the search – is something that people on the outside do not think about. It is part of the design, but it is also part of the cost.'

The provision of sanitary products in women's prisons

has historically been a contested and poorly managed area of the female estate. For much of the history of women's imprisonment, women were expected to request sanitary items from officers, an embarrassing process.

Cath, who worked at both Holloway and New Hall, recalled a practical detail that captures something of the makeshift reality of those years. 'They used tampons for nosebleeds at Holloway,' she said.

The response from some prisoners was its own form of assertion. 'Women do it where they shove dirty sanitary towels out,' Cath noted. 'Just to make a point, just to cause as much trouble and upset as they can.'

Birthdays in prison are stripped of almost everything that makes them feel like birthdays. What remains is the date itself, and the knowledge among those who share your wing of what the date means.

Anastasia spent four of her birthdays inside. 'It is just a normal day,' she told us. 'But some of the girls would wrap me presents up from the Avon catalogue or canteen in newspaper. They'd find something – a lip balm, a shower gel, something off their own canteen sheet – and they'd wrap it up in newspaper and write on it. That was the gift. And it meant something, because they didn't have anything either. They were giving you a piece of what little they had.'

Eleanor spent her birthday inside on her first sentence, and had not anticipated managing it with any grace. 'I was on an education course – about ten of us in the class. And the girls had asked me, do you like cheesecake? And this girl – she'd bought the cream, and the biscuits, and the chocolate, and everything, to make me a cheesecake for my birthday. I barely knew her, we were just on the same wing. Obviously I wasn't going to eat it in my room on my own. You've got your ID card, same size as a credit card – no knives or forks in the class. I said to the girls, just scoop it out on your ID cards, and I shared it round the room. Nobody's got any money in there. Nobody's better off than anyone else in that sense. So to have done that – oh, it was just the sweetest thing.'

Christmas at Askham Grange open prison was a different kind of experience from anything else Eleanor had known inside. 'It looks like a big country house. You could go in your pyjamas into the corridors, and people were saying, Merry Christmas, Merry Christmas. The staff served our dinner. The best thing was the church and the primary school from the village had made us little gift bags – Radox shower gel, a bag of sweets. It was so impressive. That was nice. At New Hall, Christmas is no different to a Saturday. You're banged behind your door. No staff because everyone's on holiday. But at Askham, it was actually Christmas.'

For Neah, the birthday that sent her to prison was her 18th.

Every occasion that brings something into the prison – a visit, a delivery, a festival food package, a birthday parcel, a chaplaincy basket – also brings with it the possibility of something else arriving alongside it. Everything that gets in is a potential carrier. What comes in, and how, is the subject of the next chapter.

CHAPTER 12

Contraband

'We used to dry out banana skins on the radiator,
because it gives you a little bit of a high. And we would
sniff the bleach from the cleaning products.'
ANASTASIA SEVERN

In women's prisons, the contraband landscape differs in some respects from the male estate. Violence in pursuit of drug debts is less common, though not absent. The methods of concealment tend towards the improvised rather than the industrial. And the range of items that qualify as contraband is broader than the public generally understands: phones, SIM cards, chargers, prescription medication, alcohol, unauthorised vapes, and the synthetic cannabinoids collectively known as spice are all as significant in the women's estate as the drugs the tabloid coverage tends to focus on.

Drugs, phones and homemade alcohol have been long-term features of prison life; the methods of concealment and delivery have evolved with the technology available on the outside.

Hooch – prison-made alcohol – has been a fixture of institutional life for as long as institutions have existed.

Neah described the method to us with the matter-of-fact precision of someone who has seen it many times. 'You save your fruit from dinner, any bits of sugar from canteen,' she told us. 'You put it all in a little mixing bowl. You tie it up in a bin bag and put the bin bag at the bottom of your bin, underneath the bin bag in your room. And it ferments. A few days later you've got some sort of drink. You add a bit of Marmite for the yeast. And everyone knew what was going on. It's not like you can keep it secret, because it smells. But if everyone on the landing is turning a blind eye, it doesn't much matter.'

She had hooch on the go in every prison she was ever in, she told us. 'I always had hooch on,' she said. 'Whatever prison I was in, whatever landing, I always had a brew going. The best jobs are the wing worker jobs because you're out on the wing all day, you can handle the kitchen, you can see when the officers are coming, and you're the one emptying the bins, so you can keep things in there that no one else is going to touch. You put the hooch in a rubbish bag inside the bin. Five litres of washing-up liquid bowls from the kitchen. You put loads of Marmite in it; Marmite is really good for the yeast. Loads of fruit, sometimes boiled, apples and oranges. Loads of sugar. Leave it for a week, open it slowly each day just to let the air out. Ends up like a violent brandy. Really aggressive stuff.'

Anastasia had made hooch at Eastwood Park and been

caught. 'We had it in a Lucozade bottle under the sink,' she told us. 'It was actually pretty obvious. But for a while it worked.' On the subject of improvised intoxication more broadly, she was direct. 'We used to eat the banana skins at Eastwood Park. I kid you not. You dry them out on the radiator. Because it gives you a little bit of a high. And we'd sniff the bleach from the cleaning products. When there is nothing else and your brain is craving something, anything, you find out what's available and you use it.'

Suzy had worked at HMP Dartmoor early in her cross-sex deployment, and the contrast with what she had seen in the women's estate in terms of hooch production was striking. She indicated to us that at Dartmoor the men had organised operations. Proper fermentation set-ups, it was quite sophisticated. The women tend to be more improvised about it. Opportunistic rather than industrialised. As she said 'which doesn't mean it doesn't work.' It just means it's different in scale and ambition.

She also recalled an incident at Dartmoor that illustrated the capacity of confined, bored men and women to find uses for contraband that no one had anticipated. 'One of the prisoners had been caught brewing rice wine,' she told us. 'They found it in his cell – it was a gallon container, it was rice, and it was blowing away nicely, getting quite alcoholic. The staff had found it and they brought it into the office to use as evidence for the adjudication. But they left it on the hot water pilot. And so by the time they came back the next morning, it had exploded and completely pebble-dashed the office in this alcoholic rice. The smell was there for weeks.' The women, she said, were equally ingenious, and still are.

In the early years of New Hall as a women's prison, the problem was already present, if less sophisticated in its organisation. Bev Butler described a discovery during a cell search that illustrated the basic principle: wait, watch and confiscate before anyone realises what you have found. 'One time there were what we called the dorms,' she told us. 'There would be, like, five inmates in one room. And they'd all gone to dinner. So while they'd gone to dinner, we had a quick search of one of the rooms, and on the windowsill was a spoon with what looked like heroin or something, you know, dried. They'd obviously heated it in some way. And then so what we did was we took the spoon away and whatever else we could find, and didn't say anything to them. Just let them back in after dinner and stood at the door, and you'd hear them looking for it.'

The incoming search was the first line of defence, and it was not always adequate. The concealment women were capable of on arrival was illustrated earlier by Bev's account of finding a razor blade lodged in a woman's cheek during a reception search at New Hall. What arrived through reception was only part of the picture.

The drug landscape itself had shifted dramatically over the years Nicola Webster had worked in the prison. When she had started, it was different in kind as much as degree. 'Spice wasn't in the prison when I was there,' she said. 'They made hooch on the radiators with sugar and orange and stuff like that, make basic sort of alcoholic stuff. But I mean, they could crush any tablet, really, and the way that they get it in, they put it on stamps and paper and all this sort of thing. But I would love to know what an induction course in the prison entails now, because I reckon there's a massive emphasis on drugs. There are drones and that now. We never had drones. Yeah, drones over the prison fence, dropping stuff in. I've just been on a friend's birthday party with ten prison officers that I haven't seen for 20 years. And the stories they told me now are just horrific.'

Nicola, speaking from the healthcare side, was straight with us about the challenge that the female body presented for security – and about one memorable occasion when the problem resolved itself rather unexpectedly. 'The female body is well made for hiding stuff, isn't it?' she said. 'So you can't, we can't search anybody. We can't. I mean, this is another story. We used to have a lady that comes in doing gynaecological examinations, and this one day she couldn't get the speculum up, and the inmate went, "oh, shit, I forgot to take the drugs out, Miss."'

'From a medical perspective, we had to be careful what we prescribe for patients,' she added. 'We had dissolvable paracetamol for people. Well, apparently you can turn that into a bomb because of the effervescence of it. Certain medication, like temazepam, we used to have capsules. Well, you can get the liquid out of the middle and inject it, and whatever thing you can imagine to do with anything a prisoner will have thought about it. There was a hatch where the pharmacy was. What the doctor used to do was hand the prescription to the patient. Well, this lady obviously came with a crutch pen somewhere, and added to the prescription. So those are the sorts of things.'

Drugs enter women's prisons through a variety of routes, and the routes have changed significantly in the past decade. The traditional choke points – visits, reception, incoming mail – remain relevant. Drones and the practice of throwing packages over the perimeter wall have added new vectors that no amount of gate security can fully address.

Neah described the throwing operation at Styal with a specificity that suggested it was not an occasional occurrence. 'There were people on the outside – Frog was one of them – who used to throw packages over the wall,' she told us. 'You'd be on the exercise yard and something would come over. And everyone knew. The screws knew, but they couldn't always stop it. Frog was reliable. You could get a message out through a visitor and Frog would deliver. It was a service.'

The operation was more elaborate than it might appear. 'Frog used to bring me stuff up in an orange and throw it over the wall. I couldn't believe someone could do it like that. They're called throwers. It's a proper job description. Lots of skill. You just get better and better and you're a professional thrower. Whatever you asked for, whatever you needed. Phones, whatever. He was really active, the guy. Obviously you'd have to throw it in a place where you could benefit, and you've got to get it before someone else does. Sometimes it gets confiscated, sometimes someone else picks it up. But it was worth it because whatever I'd get put in there would make way more back.'

Phones were ubiquitous, whatever the regulations said. 'The phones, you're not allowed them, but most people have them,' she said. 'The little ones, just ones that make calls, they're best because you can hide them. You've got to also hide a charger but it's just a little USB lead you plug into the back of the TV, so it's easy. You charge it, hide it, and you're sorted. I did get caught once. But the amount of times I got through without being caught, it was worth the risk.'

Suzy described how drones had transformed the situation in the years before her retirement. 'Drones have completely changed the contraband landscape,' she told us. 'The traditional choke points – visits, reception, mail – have all been partially circumvented. You find packages in the exercise yard, on the roof, in the gardens. And the items coming in are more sophisticated now too. It's not just drugs. It's phones, chargers, SIM cards, vapes. The technology of delivery has kept pace with the technology of the products.'

Spice – synthetic cannabinoid – has been one of the most significant developments in prison drug culture in the last decade. It is cheap, potent, difficult to detect, and can be dissolved into a liquid and sprayed on to paper, making it almost invisible to conventional search methods.

Eleanor observed the geography of spice use on the wings with the precise attention of someone who had learned to read the social landscape of the institution from the ground up. 'At the minute in women's jails they've got spice. They smoke it in the showers. The shower block on some wings is communal – like swimming pool cubicles, with big gaps in the doors, so you can see everything. Some girls go to the shower and you just know. It's stronger than cannabis – you can get it for next to nothing in there. The hallucinations are mad. I saw one girl come back on to the wing holding on to the wall for dear life, completely gone; every time she moved going, "fire in the hole." It was everywhere, and staff couldn't get on top of it.'

The BOSS chair – Body Orifice Security Scanner – sits in reception in prisons that have them, scanning for metal items concealed internally. It is an effective tool but it is not a complete solution. 'Women have found ways around it,' Suzy told us simply. 'They know to go to the toilet before they sit on it. They know where the sensor is less sensitive. Anything that can be circumvented will be circumvented, given enough time and enough motivation. And the motivation is always there.'

The search technology had improved but remained imperfect. 'You go through a pretty thorough search,' she said. 'You've got the BOSS chair. But you've got hundreds of people coming through reception and you can still get things through. Stuff comes through the post. With a lot of synthetic drugs they're so hard to detect. Stuff gets sent in on paper. You just need to drop a few drops of something on a piece of paper and you can't see it and you can't detect it until you burn it, and then it's ferocious stuff.'

The drones compounded the problem further during

her time. 'Drones were just starting,' she said. 'You can spot them over the prison and report them, but you know, you can get a drone for £25 on Amazon now. It's as easy as bouncing a tennis ball over the wall and into the garden. If it's coming from somebody who knows the prison, they'll know exactly what's on the other side of the fence at what point, because they've been in the prison. They're not randomly throwing something and hoping someone picks it up.'

The logical conclusion, she noted, admitted no comfortable resolution. 'The only way to stop drugs coming in entirely is to keep people in complete isolation from any human contact, which is unrealistic and inhumane.'

One of the less visible vectors for contraband was the short-term recall. Women who committed minor offences and were recalled to custody on licence breaches were, in some cases, using the journey back in as a delivery mechanism. Suzy described what this looked like in practice.

'The short-termers who get recalled – some of them have found a way to monetise it,' she told us. 'They'll go out, pick up a package, and come back in. The package comes with them. Their recall is a delivery service. It is a business model. For people with very limited options on the outside, it is actually a rational one. You know you're going back in. You might as well earn from the journey.'

The scale of the problem was significant. 'Phones and drugs,' she said. 'The short-term recalls have been an absolute bloody nightmare, to be honest. A woman who's been in and out of prison a dozen, 20, 30, 40 times, going in on a two-week recall is just like a business opportunity. They come in packed. Women have orifices that men don't have, and they will come through reception loaded with drugs, distribute them, have a bit of a chat, couple of weeks later they're gone. They know how to do it. It's nothing, is it? Going into a prison you've been in 20 times before.'

The most consequential source of contraband, and the most difficult to address, is not the clever concealment or the drone or the throwing arm outside the wall. It is the officer who brings things in.

Neah described the process by which staff were drawn into the supply chain with an uncomfortable precision. 'It's a whole operation,' she told us. 'It's not like you walk up to someone and go, "Will you bring me in drugs?" It's a whole grooming process. You become their friend. You find out about their life. You ask about their family, their problems, their money. You make them feel seen. You make them feel special. And then one day you ask. And they don't want to say no, because by then they feel like they know you. By then they've already crossed so many small lines that one more doesn't feel like much. That's how it works. It's very sophisticated. It takes months. Some of the women in there are running operations that any business school would recognise.'

The targeting of staff was, she said, its own parallel operation, often conducted collectively and with a clear objective. 'On Bronzefield we'd sit in a cell as a group when a new male officer came on to the wing, and we'd work out who he was most likely to be attracted to, and then get her to come on to him. Not for anything serious, just to get him where we wanted him. Someone would say, "I think he likes you, no it's not me, no it's not me," someone else would go, "right, I'll take one for the team." Because all you're thinking is, can we get that bottle of brandy for Saturday? Who's going to get it to us the quickest? And if something was going on between an officer and a prisoner, other prisoners would know, and then put pressure on the officer. "What are you getting us? Because if you're not getting anything, what are you doing?" It sounds calculating, and it was. But it's also just survival, and what passes for entertainment when that's the world you're in.'

Kay Lumb described a case that illustrated the creativity applied to concealment at the individual level. One prisoner, she told us, a drug addict, was a regular subject of suspicion but consistently came up clean on searches. 'She was a drug addict and a nice person, and she had been bringing cannabis in for who knows how long.' Her method was eventually revealed.

'I was on visits and I saw this visitor who came in fiddling with his wrist. I saw a prisoner take it off him. She fiddled with his watch strap. I didn't even have to strip search. She said, "It's here." It was cannabis.'

The introduction of in-cell telephones, Suzy noted, had an unexpected effect on some areas of the contraband market. 'When women could phone their children from their own cell at night, the appetite for smuggled phones dropped,' she told us. 'Not to zero – there are things you can do on a smartphone that you can't do on a monitored landline. But the desperation to have a phone – to be able to say goodnight, to be reachable in an emergency – that particular desperation was addressed. If you meet a legitimate need, you reduce the pressure in that part of the system. It is not a complicated principle, but it took a long time to apply.'

The benefit was visible to those who worked on the wings. 'Women genuinely appreciate the in-cell phones,' she said. 'They can have private conversations. They can say goodnight to their children during lock-up. They're not queuing on a landing to use a public phone. I think that's taken a lot of the heat off wanting contraband phones, to be honest. The calls are a small percentage monitored, all intelligence led. The vast majority of women who have that privilege wouldn't abuse it, because they wouldn't want it taken away. They want it legitimately, to say goodnight to their kids. Anything that can be done to mitigate their suffering around that separation has to be a good thing.'

The flow of contraband is driven, at its root, by the same need that drives everything else in these places: the need for connection with the world on the other side of the wall.

CHAPTER 13

Prison Visits & Transfers

'It is not like booking into the nearest Premier Inn.
They do not ask you where you would like to go.'
YVONNE SIMPSON

The movement of prisoners – to court, to hospital, between establishments, into and out of custody – is one of the least visible dimensions of the system and one of the most human.

When a woman is told she is being transferred, she is rarely given much notice and never given much choice.

The geographical reality of the women's estate – 12 prisons serving the whole of England, one each in Scotland and Northern Ireland, and none in Wales – means that distance is built into every transfer.

Suzy had spent her career watching this from the other side of the door. 'If they close Eastwood Park, which covers something like seven or eight counties, from Cornwall to mid-Wales to the Midlands,' she said, 'if you live in West Cornwall and you get sent to prison, you're going to go to probably Derbyshire. Some of the women don't even know where that is because they've not been very far from their homes before. And it's not just your family that can't visit you. Your probation officer and your job seeking and all that stuff is completely blown out of the water.'

She gave us a case that made the human cost of the system's indifference to geography concrete. 'I had a case where a woman had a very young baby,' she said. 'The baby was young enough to come into the prison, and she could have had the baby with her on the mother and baby unit. But she also had slightly older children, still at primary school age. To go to the mother and baby unit, she'd have had to move about 200 miles from her home. So the choice was: move 200 miles and keep her baby with her but not see the older children, or give up the baby and have the family brought in on regular visits. I believe no woman should have to make that choice. That is a reality.'

For the women on the receiving end of visits, the process of getting family through the gates was its own ordeal. Yvonne described it without sentimentality. 'The visits are as hard as the absence,' she told us. 'You want to see your kids but it is also difficult. Social workers were bringing some of mine and I felt watched and assessed the entire time. There is no privacy. For women coming in from outside, the search process alone is humiliating enough that by the time they reach you, they have already been through something. It traumatises the families as much as the prisoners. And when the visit ends and you have to say good-bye again, that is some of the hardest moments in there.'

Neah passed through eight establishments over the course of her sentence. We asked her to rank them. She did not hesitate. 'Downview was my first, the day I turned 18. Then Holloway when I was 19. Bronzefield at 22. Then Peterborough. Back to Bronzefield again. Then Foston Hall. Then HMP Styal. Drake Hall. HMP Send. Eight out of ten. The best is Drake Hall. You wouldn't even believe you're in prison up there. They don't lock you in. Little houses, like a small estate. It's in Staffordshire and I think it used to be an open prison. Then they just put gates around it. It still has that open prison vibe. The worst is Styal. The bang-up is rough. The banging and echoing at night from pipes is really awful. One time I didn't get a shower for five days. Legally you're meant to get one once a week but even that was often not happening. Frogs in the shower. The drugs are really, really bad up there, and the officers just use it as an excuse not to engage. Someone's smoking spice, they're going home. So you don't get out much. You don't get your medication on time. Really rough.'

The court run is the most regular form of movement in the Prison Service's daily life and generates its own culture.

Cath Thompson had done hundreds of court runs and described their texture with the amusement of someone who had seen most things twice. 'It's surreal, the court run,' she told us. 'You spend all this time looking after them on the wing, and then you're out in the world with them, and they're just people. Nervous people going to a court hearing. You stop for breakfast on the way. They want a bacon sandwich. You want a bacon sandwich. You sit opposite each other at a service station table and you have a bacon sandwich.'

Cath had been in the dock during the sentencing of a pregnant shoplifter who, after going down, told her family the judge had accused her of getting pregnant to avoid a custodial sentence. He had not. 'He turned around and said, I do not know if you have got yourself pregnant to stop yourself being sent down,' Cath told us. 'But: and we were actually in the back of a taxi, Wakefield rank, on the way back, and we were pictured on Granada News, me and her looking back at the window, because they were filming there.'

'I was sat in the dock with her when he said it,' Cath said. The remark Cath had to relay to the solicitor was the actual one: he had said he did not know whether she had got herself pregnant to stop herself being sent down, and he had said it whether she was pregnant or not, she deserved to be sent down. Debbie found the court run an occasion that contained, alongside the work itself, an oddly civilised set of rituals for the officers escorting prisoners. 'Lunchtime was always a big thing,' she told us, 'because if it was a really nice area, you could go out at lunchtime and do some shopping. And it was like a day out, really. The court staff used to cook you a big fry-up at breakfast when you got in. It was like a day out. You had a cooked breakfast, then shopping at lunchtime. We'd come back with loads of shopping bags and try and hide them. Thinking, don't get caught.'

The prisoner was in court for the day. The officers waited, escorted, supervised, and at lunchtime, if the court was somewhere with a high street, went and did the shopping they couldn't fit into a normal week. The contrast between what the woman in the dock was facing and what the officers were doing fifty yards away in Marks & Spencer is the kind of thing that prison work routinely produces and that nobody outside it ever quite imagines.

Suzy described what those journeys gave her that the wing never could. 'You get to know someone very differently in a car than on a wing,' she told us. 'On the wing, you're always the officer. In a car on the M1 for three hours, you're just two people. They talk about their families. About what they're hoping for at court. About what they'll do if they get out. Some of those conversations have stayed with me longer than almost anything that happened in a prison building.'

Simon described what he considered the most surreal assignment of his escorting career: the Isle of Wight ferry run. It was, when he told us about it, the story that made us understand most clearly what this work involves. 'You put the prisoner in civilian clothes, you're in civilian clothes, you're handcuffed to them, and you get on the public ferry,' he said. 'And there are families, pushchairs, people on holiday. And you're just standing there with this person attached to your wrist. Some of them took it brilliantly. One prisoner I escorted we bought an ice cream. Just stood there on the deck eating an ice cream, handcuffed to me, watching the Solent go by. And I thought: this is the job. This is genuinely the job. There is nothing in any training programme that prepares you for escorting a lifer through a crowd of day-trippers while they eat a Cornetto.'

He described the prisoner escort record – the PER – as the document that governed every journey, requiring a descriptive entry of the prisoner's state every 15 minutes.

The most demanding escort Kay undertook was of a different order from anything else she described to us. 'I wouldn't uncuff her because she was too dangerous. She had cut her arm off.' We asked Kay to describe the practicalities of moving someone in that condition, and what she gave us was not a description of procedure but of a person. 'Rampton escort, three if not four of us, an SO and three officers. I was cuffed to her. When we were on the minibus I sat so she couldn't throw a punch. She was nice to staff, she just hated herself. She was quite sexually abused as a child by her own father and family; she thought she was a bad person because she was abused.'

Kay had the memorable experience of escorting Beverley Allitt to hospital.

Her care was not necessarily received with gratitude, as Kay noted wryly. 'When She said: "Oh, no not you."

I thought: that's rich. We're there to look after you, we're the ones sitting outside the curtain for six hours, and that's your response: not you again. But there it is. That's the escort. You don't get to choose who you're grateful to.'

The second visit was of a different order. Allitt had been admitted having been found to be vomiting faeces, a condition attributed to self-inflicted anorexia, and was threatening to kill herself. Kay spent a week of nights on escort duty at the hospital. 'Me and a male officer had to sit there all night so she didn't kill herself. We had a police officer too. She went, "Oh no, not you." She was in a side room off the ward. She didn't sleep much. She was on a closeting chain. That's when you take a prisoner in cuffs and a long chain with a cuff on each end. I was cuffed to the other. She could get to the loo. She denied her crimes. Said, "I haven't done that to all them babies."

'She came in quite plump. When I did the nights on her, she had faeces under her fingernails. She rang her buzzer. She was vomiting faeces. She hadn't been to the loo one night. I was playing Sudoku and felt tired. She sat bolt upright in bed and started screaming. It started as a scream and went into a laugh. There was a screech of brakes that came just at that time and she said, "Have they come for me?" She was petrified. Her behaviour changed. I didn't hold conversations with her. She knew she couldn't manipulate me. Some staff feel a bit sorry for people. She's still in Rampton. I don't think she was mentally ill. Beverley Allitt wanted to be the most notorious female prisoner. She said after she was arrested, "Well, everybody will know me now."'

Bev's Rampton escort had a different quality. The woman she was taking had been held in a Doncaster mental health unit, assessed as no longer a danger, released, and within days had stabbed someone at the Frenchgate Centre in the town. She was quiet on the journey. At Rampton, Bev and her colleagues were shown around while the handover was completed. 'We got to the swimming pool, a big swimming pool, and there was an inmate in the shallow end. A big lass just stood there. We stood watching her for a while. There were PE staff and other staff around, and they were going, "Come on out, come on out." And she was going, "No. You've got to come in and get me." They were going, "We're not coming in, we want you to come out." They took ages. She was not coming out without a fight. So they had a dance.'

The question of how the woman had been cleared for release in the first place had its own bleak answer. 'The medical notes from the secure unit she'd been in before hadn't been forwarded on to us, and Rampton had quite a job getting them,' Bev told us. 'Everybody's theory was that it was a cover-up, because after their disaster with her she'd managed to go out and stab someone, and nobody wanted that on paper.'

Debbie described her own experience of escorting a woman to Rampton. 'She was quite volatile,' she told us. 'On the way there we stopped at a services that had a swimming pool attached. And she wanted to go swimming.' Debbie paused. We waited. 'And I thought – well, she's not sectioned yet. She's not formally detained under the Mental Health Act. We can't really say no outright. So she went swimming. This girl who had just stabbed someone in a shopping centre went swimming at a motorway services. And then we got her to Rampton and handed her over.'

Yvonne had been on the receiving end of what the escort relationship could look like at its worst, with a certain type of officer. 'It's like being a housemistress at a boarding school,' she said. 'You might be okay, but there's also a higher chance than usual that you might be in this for the wrong reasons, because what a great opportunity, if you wanted to use it for the wrong reasons. If you're power-hungry and have some kind of fantasy wielding power over vulnerable people.'

The officer she described had used the management of a personal letter – a letter for another prisoner, Jo, about adoption – as a demonstration of that power. 'Jo said, "Please have the letter." And the officer said, "You're really going to have to wait until I'm done, aren't you, girls?" Oh yeah. All weekend. It's just awful.'

Bev was direct about what the Rampton runs had taught her. 'Rampton is where you go when the prison can't manage you any more,' she told us. 'And the people you're taking there – you understand why, by the time you get to the gate. You understand why Rampton exists.'

The movement of prisoners through the system exposes, more clearly than almost any other aspect of custody, the gap between what the institution says it is and what it actually is. What happens on the way to court or in a hospital ward is candid in a way the wing rarely is. What happens on the wing, beneath the surface of the routine, is a different kind of candour entirely.

CHAPTER 14

Mind Games

'You would be amazed at the number of officers who have lost their jobs, their marriages, their homes. Because of what happens in those four walls. And it starts so small that no one can pinpoint when it became something else.'
SUZY DYMOND-WHITE

As we have learned in all our previous book research, the enclosed environment of a prison produces a specific and unique psychology of power. Everyone inside – officers and prisoners alike – is operating within a hierarchy that is total in its reach and inescapable in its daily application. The prisoner has no power over where she sleeps, what she eats, when she can use the phone, whether her letter arrives today or next week. The officer controls all of this. The officer, in turn, is subject to the governor, the area manager, the Inspectorate, the policy shift from the Ministry, the union, the shift pattern. Within this system, the manipulation of available power – by prisoners over staff, by staff over prisoners, sometimes by both simultaneously – is not an aberration. It is a feature.

A prisoner entering a new establishment has one

significant tool available to her: observation. She cannot leave, cannot choose her companions, cannot vary her day in any meaningful way. What she can do is watch. And what she watches, consistently and with great skill, is the staff.

Cath described this from the officer's side with the clarity of someone who has been watched for decades. 'They know everything about you within a week,' she told us. 'They watch you. They notice which officer you talk to most. They notice when you look tired. They notice when you seem distracted. They notice when you've had a haircut, or when you haven't. And they file it all away. Because information is currency in there. What you do with what you know determines where you sit in the social order. And the women are very, very good at it.'

The specific intelligence they gathered, she said, was not dramatic. It was domestic. 'They want to know if you're having trouble at home. If your marriage is going through something. If you're in debt. If your child is ill. They pick it up from the way you carry yourself. From a remark you make to a colleague. From the fact that you're on your phone more than usual. And once they have it, they use it. Not necessarily in a crude way. Often very subtly. They just make you feel understood. And that is the start of it.'

Suzy had seen the mechanics of inappropriate relation-ships between staff and prisoners play out across decades, and she described the process by which they began with a precision that made the progression seem almost inevitable. As she made clear and as we have seen ourselves, the grooming of prison staff follows almost exactly the same incremental logic as any other grooming process. Each step feels small. Each step feels defensible. You looked tired, she asked if you were all right, you said yes. She asked again the next day. The day after that you told her a little of what was actually wrong. And you felt better for having told her. And she felt closer to you. And you felt, without being able to articulate it, that you owed her something. It is a very old mechanism.

Not all manipulation operates at this level of sophistication. Cath described how an officer going through difficulties at home became immediately visible to the wing. 'The women notice straight away,' she said. 'An officer who's just separated from his wife will suddenly have a woman who's never spoken to him before making him a cup of tea. Asking him about his weekend. Showing concern. And he thinks: she's nice. She's the only one who's asked. And it has begun.'

Suzy had known cases throughout her career, and she described the pattern with an even-handedness that did not excuse but did explain. 'I knew an officer – a very decent officer, actually – who had a perfectly good marriage, a perfectly good home, two children,' she told us. 'And became increasingly involved with a long-term prisoner. Not sexually, to begin with. Just present. Always finding reasons to be on that wing. Always the one who dealt with her. And then it became something else. And by the time it became something else, he had already crossed so many lines that he couldn't go back. He lost his job. He lost his marriage. His wife left and took the children. He ended up in a flat. And the prisoner was eventually transferred. So he lost everything, and she lost nothing. That is one version of how it goes.'

It starts, she said, with a vulnerability, and women see it immediately. 'It happens,' she told us. 'It tends to happen when the member of staff shows a vulnerability. Women are incredibly clever and they just see a chink in the armour and they're straight in. I had a very sad case of an officer I'd known for years; I'd known him in a male prison. He came to a female prison. He was a vulnerable character. He went through a divorce and my understanding is that he somehow let it be known he was going through a tricky time. I think one of the female prisoners asked him to bring her in a book or something. And once you've brought them in one thing, they go, unless you bring me the next thing, we're going to tell on the first thing. And this is how it builds. In the end, she asked him to meet her on release and this relationship started. He was still a serving officer. He furnished her flat, bought her a car, set her and her kids up, absolutely believing it was going to flourish. She then took everything and finished the relationship and wrote to the prison laying it all out. We received the letter. I had to dismiss him. He had lost his home, his wife, his job, and the relationship he thought he had. We were genuinely worried about whether he would take his own life at one point.'

The point at which the situation could have been corrected was the very beginning, she said, and the institutional mechanisms for doing so existed – if only officers used them. 'What he should have done at the very beginning was report it,' Suzy told us. 'Said, she's asking me to bring this in. Put it into security. We would have made sure he worked somewhere where he didn't come into contact with her. We could have moved her to a different prison. We could have moved him off operational duties temporarily and said, "you're too vulnerable at the moment." There are a lot of things you can do, but not if people don't tell you what's going on. Once somebody starts off down the wrong track, it's very difficult to come back.'

Naivety was not confined to the male estate or to romantic entanglements. 'I had another case in a male prison, completely naive,' Suzy said. 'One of the caterers was a civilian, and she offered a lifer her home address to go for his home leave. I spoke to her and I said, "do you realise the implications? You've got young children. You only know what he told you his crime was. He's serving a life sentence, it's not shoplifting." She was completely taken in. He'd promised her this and that. I said, "social services will be all over you and your children." Very sad, actually. Some people are just so naive.'

The cohesion of the staff group itself was, in her view, the most effective structural protection against all of this. 'If your staff group aren't tight as a group, then they are more vulnerable,' she said. 'Everybody needs to feel part of the gang. If you have a staff group that aren't cohesive, they're more likely to look for an allegiance elsewhere. A good strong union is good for me as a governor, because they pull people together. You can work with them, and you know that the staff group will feel part of something, which makes them less likely to look for that elsewhere.'

She was clear to us about the asymmetry. 'The prisoner almost always has more to gain and less to lose,' she said. 'She is already in prison. Her life is already constrained in every direction. An alliance with a member of staff gives her access to things she cannot otherwise have. For the officer, the risk is total. His career, his family, his reputation, his freedom in some cases. And yet it happens, over and over. Because the need to be needed is a very powerful thing. In a women's prison, where the women are very good at making you feel needed, it is a particularly dangerous environment for someone who is going through something difficult at home.'

The abuse of power does not only flow in one direction.

Yvonne described a specific type of officer, one she had encountered more than once across her sentence, who used the exercise of ordinary duties as an opportunity for the demonstration of control. 'There was one officer who was just power-hungry,' she told us. 'You know the type. You'd ask for the most basic thing – a sanitary towel, a paracetamol, a form – and she'd make you wait. Not because there weren't any. Not because she was busy. Just to make you wait. Because she could. Because for those 30 seconds, she had all the power and you had none.

And you could see her enjoying it. That small pleasure of making someone else stand there. And you couldn't say anything, because then you'd be the difficult one, and it would be worse the next time.'

The cruelty of this dynamic, she said, was that it was invisible. 'There is nothing to report. She didn't do anything wrong, technically. She gave you what you asked for. Eventually. She just made you feel it first. And she knew exactly what she was doing. That kind of officer exists in every prison. They are not in it for the rehabilitation, they are in it for the power. And in a women's prison, where the women are already some of the most vulnerable and least powerful people in the country, that is a very bad combination.'

The control of correspondence was another instrument. Yvonne described a specific incident in which a letter – something that mattered to her, that she had been waiting for – was held back without explanation and delivered days later, with no apology and no acknowledgement of the delay. 'You can't prove it was deliberate,' she told us. 'That's the point. You can't prove any of it. The waiting, the small humiliations, the way certain officers look at you when you ask for something you are entitled to. None of it is provable. All of it is real.'

Kay placed this vulnerability in a broader structural context, drawing on her own experience of a working environment where the rules were not always enforced or even acknowledged. 'Prisoners have an ability to seek your weaknesses out,' she said. 'Staff who had overstepped the mark, if they had an inappropriate relationship, it was swept under the carpet. I was quite fortunate because I was very loud. If something was wrong, I could speak up. I had a different relationship with the inmates because I was a PE instructor. I never let anybody cross the line. I knew the prisoners.'

Nicola described the dynamic that developed when high-profile prisoners wanted to discuss their crimes, and the deliberate strategy she adopted in response. 'Yes, they love talking about the crimes,' she said. 'And I used to just say, "now I'm not here to talk about that." And often you'd get high-profile cases. If I was working on the segregation unit, and somebody would come in because they were going to the local court, so they'd be transferred. If they were on the telly, they'd start talking about it, and I would just ignore it. Not make a big thing of it, because they're wanting that gratitude and that glory, aren't they?'

Eleanor described an incident that illustrated both how quickly a formal grievance could be manufactured inside a prison, and how much depended on which officer happened to be paying attention. 'I was in reception using my phone – the officer on duty had allowed me to get it out to send payslips to the employment club. This other officer came in and sat right next to me, asked what I was doing. I told him. An hour later I was walking down the corridor and an officer I trusted pulled me aside. He said, "you need to be really careful with him. He's put in an intelligence report saying you've said something, and it's gone up to security." I said, "do you want to see the actual email?" He knew I was telling the truth. And it turned out the senior officer had already had the report pulled. He told me – off the record – that he'd gone to security and said, "do you honestly think she meant that? Let's recognise what needs dealing with and what doesn't." He shouldn't have told me any of it. But he was just being sound. That's the full range in there. You get both types.'

Bev recalled with good humour the challenge presented by a transgender prisoner arriving in reception, and the discovery that followed a strip search that had missed something significant. 'Oh, another time,' she said, 'we had this woman, or man, come in. Two staff strip-searched her, as always two staff in the strip-searching. And then they came into the main reception bit, and I receptioned this one and put, you know, everything on paper; I wrote everything down. Found her a place. She had to go on the hospital wing to start with. Most of them did, not all of them. Anyway, the doctor rang down to reception the next morning and said, "who searched this woman last night?" Why? "He's got a willy." They hadn't noticed in the strip search. What happened? She stayed with us. It was only short term, I think it was maybe a week or two. It was very sad, actually, because she'd had a relationship with a man, as her being a woman, and he used to beat her and was terrible to her. We said, "do you want us to send her to a male jail and get the same treatment again?" So we kept her. At that stage, definitely, if a trans prisoner went to a male jail there'd be a real risk of attack. This one couldn't stand up for herself. She was definitely vulnerable.'

What distinguished the most effective officers from the least, across the testimony of every contributor to all our *Inside . . .* books, was not physical strength or procedural knowledge or seniority. It was the ability to read the room – to understand what the wing was, who the key players were, what the current tensions were, and how to move through all of it without either being manipulated or becoming manipulative.

Suzy reckons this can only be learned through experience. 'You can walk on a wing and feel that something isn't right,' she told us. 'You couldn't point to it, but you know. And that knowing – that jailcraft – is what keeps people safe. The officers who don't have it are the ones who end up in trouble. Not because they are bad people. Because they cannot read what is happening around them. And in that environment, not reading what is happening around you is very dangerous.'

The flip side of that competence, she added, was knowing your own vulnerabilities. 'Every officer has them,' she said. 'The ones who last are the ones who know what theirs are. They know what they are susceptible to. They know when they are starting to feel something they shouldn't. And they take themselves off that wing, or they talk to someone, or they do something about it before it becomes something they can't undo. The ones who don't know their own vulnerabilities – those are the ones you read about.'

The psychological landscape of the prison – the reading of power, the management of need, the ongoing negotiation between those who hold authority and those who must navigate it – is the context within which the most extreme events occur. Violence in a women's prison does not arrive without warning. It arrives out of that landscape, from pressures that have been building in exactly the ways this chapter has described.

CHAPTER 15

Riots, Violence & Escape Attempts

*'She had filed the radiator fins down to points and
fashioned them into claws. Like Freddy Krueger.
It took three teams of staff before we got her down.'*
SIMON PETERS

Violence in women's prisons is a subject that invites an amusing misrepresentation, in both directions. The tabloid version – catfights, hysteria, the stock footage of women's wing chaos – sensationalises what is, in its daily texture, more insidious and less spectacular than the male estate equivalent. The counter-narrative, which emphasises the vulnerability of the women's population and the relative rarity of serious physical violence, risks minimising what is genuinely severe when it occurs. The reality, as almost every contributor described it, is that violence in women's prisons tends to be less frequent than in male establishments, more emotionally loaded in its origins, more likely to be turned inward, and, when it does turn outward, no less dangerous for the staff managing it.

The statistics bear this out partially. Assaults in women's prisons run consistently lower than in equivalent male establishments. But self-harm rates run consistently higher – dramatically higher – and the line between self-harm and harm to others is not always as clear as the categories suggest. A woman in acute crisis who has already cut herself and is now turning on the officer who has entered the cell is generating a statistic in each column simultaneously.

The Risley riot is described in the Prologue, in Kay Lumb's own words. The violence that punctuates daily life in a women's prison is rarely the set-piece confrontation of the kind the male estate generates. It is more likely to be sudden, personal and explosive out of an accumulation of pressures that have been building for days or weeks in an environment from which there is no exit.

Anastasia described the atmosphere on E Wing at Eastwood Park with a directness that left no room for softening. 'E Wing was the biggest wing there, and a lot of sugar and water assaults would happen on E Wing,' she told us. 'You boil the water and dissolve as much sugar as you can in it. It sticks when it hits. It burns, and it keeps burning. I saw it happen. It was terrifying – not just for the person it happened to, but for everyone on the wing. Because you knew, after you'd seen it once, that it was possible. That someone near you was capable of that.' Nits, she said, were rife throughout the wing. The combination of physical squalor and contained aggression created an environment she described simply as very dark.

Her first weeks at Drake Hall were defined by a close, nameless quality of threat. It was difficult to hear her talk about it.

'My first two or three weeks were horrendous,' she told us. 'There was a shower incident. And then one night I woke up and my pad-mate was standing over me with something in her hand. But in the morning it was just a normal morning. That is what prison is. You have a night like that and then it is just a normal morning.'

Drake Hall's unusual physical layout – the houses in a circle, the relative freedom of movement, the absence of bars on the windows – created a surface impression that bore little relationship to the social dynamics beneath it. 'Drake Hall had gangs,' Anastasia told us. 'It had its own hierarchy. You wouldn't think it looking at the place – it's almost open. But the same structures from the outside reproduce themselves inside. The same groupings. The same debts. The same disputes. A more relaxed regime does not mean a safer social world. Sometimes it means a less visible one.'

The day-to-day management of prisoners who were a danger to others or to the fabric of the building at New Hall was something Bev described with her characteristic pragmatism. It was largely a matter of containment and boredom. 'Oh, yeah, assault others or other inmates,' she said. 'So, yeah, set fire, things like that, you know. So we just start to protect everybody from them, and then we'd open them up separate, you know. We'd open them up, give them their meal and then let them go on with it.

But there was an association yard as well. They could go outside and walk around the yard, but they were on their own so they didn't go very often, bored.'

The boundary between self-harm and violence is not always where the categories suggest it should be. Juli Flintoff described incidents at New Hall that occupied a space beyond either designation.

'I had a woman who cut all the way across her stomach and was pulling her intestines out,' she told us. By the time I got there – I have never in my life seen anything like that. She survived. I don't know how. The healthcare response was very fast.' Juli does not tell these stories dispassionately. As we know from all our staff contributors over the years, what you carry after seeing something like that is not something any training prepares you for. You go home. Your family asks how your day was. It's surreal and isolating.

There was another woman, Juli said, who died from the consequences of what she did to herself. 'She was gouging into her own muscle tissue.' She died in custody, and she used to literally gouge her muscles out. And you think: what do you do with that? What do you do when the system has failed someone that completely? When someone has been in such profound and unaddressed distress for so long that they reach that point inside a building full of people whose job it is to care for them?'

Juli told us that the prison had gone through a distressing phase of women swallowing batteries so they could go to hospital.

The prisoner she remembered most clearly was a young woman of 19 whose life had been shaped, from its earliest years, by the most extreme neglect and abuse. 'One lady, she was beautiful,' Juli said. 'One of the cells had a Perspex door. She was on 24-hour watch in there because she was constantly trying to take her own life. She was a young girl of only 19. She had been given a dog's name. She had been a twin. She was housed outside with the dogs as a child. She had an appalling life. She was taken into care when she was about seven. She was raped in care when she was 14. She had no communication skills because she had been raised by dogs. She wore a hat pulled down over her eyes. They were trying to take her son away. I went walking with her. She had inadvertently set her partner on fire. She was looking at a likely life sentence. She was really worried about a court date. She went on to a general wing. She was claustrophobic and scared to go in the van. She wanted to cut herself again. I asked to be the designated officer. They were positive. It was my day off, but they cancelled it and didn't tell me. She ended up trying to take her own life. She was on life support in the hospital. I prayed with her by her bedside.'

Cath, whose career had taken her through several serious incidents, described two that had stayed with her. The first was an escort to court. 'Taking someone into court, a prison officer got stabbed,' she said flatly. 'A lady set fire to women's toilets. Set fire to the toilets at railway stations. Arson with intent. She got sectioned in the end, sent to Rampton. C wing was for mentally disturbed people. That's where they were put. Awful to cope with. They tend to put the more experienced staff down there.'

Cath had been going into cells during incidents since 1985, and she described the physical reality of it with a frankness that made clear it never became routine.

'The adrenaline when you go into a cell during an incident – I used to hyperventilate on the way,' she told us. 'Every time. You train for it. But training doesn't prepare you for that specific walk down the corridor, knowing someone behind that door has lost control and you are the one going in. Your body does not care that you have been doing this for 20 years. It responds the same way every time. What changes is that you learn to walk through it. You hyperventilate, and you keep going.'

Cath had been at Holloway for only a month when she saw an officer's jaw broken in front of her. 'The girl that was fighting got up off the floor, swung around with her elbow and cracked this officer on the jaw and broke her jaw,' she told us. 'So that's the type of thing you go into, because they just don't want to be restrained. They don't want to be taken out of the comfort zone, which is their cell, and they don't want to be put on punishment with the governor.'

The aftermath of violent incidents was something she had learned to manage in herself over decades. 'You go home,' she said simply. 'And the next day you come back in. Because if you don't come back, you never come back. I knew officers who had one bad incident and never returned. And I understood it. But I also knew that the wing needed people who had seen it and come back. That is what experience means in this job. Not that it doesn't affect you. That you come back anyway.'

Simon told us about two prisoners at Holloway whose capacity for improvised violence was especially memorable.

He recalled one prisoner who 'had over her lengthy time in the segregation unit removed and filed the fins of the radiator down to points – like Freddy Krueger's glove, basically. Very deliberately, over a period of time, without anyone noticing what she was doing. It took three teams of staff before we got her contained. The damage those fins could do – you would not believe it from looking at a prison radiator. The ingenuity, and the patience, and the sustained intent required to make that weapon and then try and use it against staff – that is what you are dealing with in a maximum-risk female prisoner. Not less dangerous than a male equivalent. Different. But not less.'

Another prisoner's violence was less premeditated but no less alarming. 'I had a prisoner who was extremely disruptive and very violent,' Simon said. 'A destroyer of property. She once put a chair leg through the wire glass panel of my visits holding room. The staff did not want to go in. I arrived and said to her: "we are going to the seg. No fuss. Walk with me now." And fortunately, she complied. I had a reputation. Prisoners knew me before I had even met them, because other prisoners would say, "if you have got a problem or you need anything, he is the one to go and speak to". They would also say that "he is not a man to be fucked with". That reputation was hard-won and I protected it.'

One long-term segregation unit resident presented a different kind of problem as she was a prolific weapons maker. 'She made a garotte from A2 pencil stubs and some wires from inside of her radio,' Simon told us. 'And she fashioned what amounted to a crossbow from pieces of furniture, some paper and an elastic band. She was improvising weapons from the fabric of the building. When you think about the ingenuity required for that, in an environment where everything is supposed to be monitored and searched, it tells you something about what sustained motivation and patience can achieve inside a prison. We found the crossbow before she used it and it was viable. If you took a dart from it in the face through the cell door hatch, it would have really buggered up your day.'

The cases that generate the most complex emotional response for staff are those that combine extreme violence with the daily management of the women responsible for it. Juli described the burden of working alongside prisoners whose crimes she was all too aware of.

'These sisters were at New Hall. They had tortured and murdered a woman with special needs in Leeds. It went on for days. They were convicted of murder and they came to us. And you know what they've done. You read the file. You know. And then you still have to manage them. You still have to look at them every day. Unlock them, give them their meals, deal with their complaints about the canteen. And they are just – they are just there. In front of you. Ordinary, in the way that people always are when you are close to them. And the crime sits behind them the whole time, and you are not supposed to let it change how you treat them. And mostly you don't. But you never forget it.'

The use of force in women's prisons had changed substantially across Simon's career. He is a physically imposing guy, acutely aware of how he carries himself and the impact it can have when he walks into a room.

'When I started, use of force was used to restore order,' he told us. 'It was understood as a tool, to be used proportionately, but used. Now it is used almost as a last resort, which in many ways is right. The training has improved, the oversight has improved, the accountability is much greater. But it has also created a situation where staff are waiting longer before intervening, and the incidents that result are sometimes worse for it. Women in crisis can do an enormous amount of damage to themselves in the time it takes to assemble a response team, get sign-off, and go in. I have watched that happen. The paperwork around use of force is now so extensive that it acts as a deterrent to staff employing its use. That is not always a good thing for the person in the cell.'

He was direct about what the shift in culture had cost at the individual level. 'Officers who intervene early and physically are now investigated for it, even when the intervention was clearly necessary,' he said. 'And officers who wait and escalate through the approved process are protected, even when waiting made things worse. That level of scrutiny and structure does not reward good judgement. It rewards compliance with procedure. And those are not always the same thing or have the best outcome for either staff or prisoners.'

Simon, reflecting on the nature of violence and how it is managed in prison, offered a description of what 20 years in the service had done to him that was, in its own way, as revealing as any incident he described. 'I do not suffer the after-effects that some people do. This environment taught me to observe and not absorb. I have never had the debilitating PTSD and the weird long-term effects. I can sit here and talk about things I have done, things I have seen, people I genuinely liked who killed themselves, bodies I have spent time with. Dead bodies make really awful noises. As the air escapes, all of that. It is terrible. But it has not broken me. I think you either develop that capacity or you do not, and if you do not, the job will eat you alive.'

The escape plot discovered in Joanna Dennehy's diary during her time on remand has been covered in this book. It's a truly chilling example of pre-planned violence in the women's estate.

The violence of the wing is one aspect of institutional life in the women's estate. Another vibe is the intimate life of the wing, the relationships that form between women who have nothing except time and proximity, and what those relationships mean and do.

CHAPTER 16

Sex Behind Bars

'In prison, women go gay. They call it gay for the stay.
And then they come out and they are straight again.
It is just what happens.'
YVONNE SIMPSON

Intimacy does not stop at the prison gate. Gay for the stay, as memorably portrayed in both the hit Netflix series *Orange is the New Black* and Piper Kerman's prison memoir that inspired it, is definitely a thing.

As we discovered, sex in prison is both ubiquitous and officially non-existent. The institutional position in England and Wales is that consensual sex cannot occur in a custodial setting. The practical reality is that it does, across all establishments and between all combinations of prisoners and, in some cases, staff. The female estate has its own particular texture of sexual life, shaped by the specific dynamics of women living together under pressure over extended periods.

The phenomenon that prison staff and prisoners alike refer to as 'gay for the stay' is one of the best-documented features of female incarceration.

Yvonne was customarily matter-of-fact. 'In prison, women go gay. It's called "gay for the stay". And then they come out and they are straight again. It is just what happens.

Simon, who had managed women at Holloway for many years, described the same dynamic from the officer's perspective. 'A lot of women do it in prison,' he told us. 'It is not necessarily sexual, it is about closeness and bonds. Women who would never have entertained it on the outside. "Gay for the stay", as we used to say. The relationships are real while they last. Some of them last beyond the sentence. Most don't. What is consistent is the need they meet: the need to be close to someone who sees you, in a place that otherwise doesn't.'

Nicola, who worked in healthcare at New Hall for a decade, was candid about the phenomenon and equally candid about the limits of her own comprehension of it. 'There was one girl, when I first started in the prison, that had set up a love triangle because a lot of them are prison gay,' she said. 'So they go in. Which was a thing I couldn't get my head around as a newbie. I couldn't get my head around that. I'm straight myself, so I don't try to understand all that.'

Neah Tuohy had observed the same thing from inside and described the phenomenon with the matter-of-fact directness of someone who has lived it and has had to navigate its social consequences. 'The relationships that form in prison between women – they can be very intense,' she told us. 'Because you have nothing else. Your whole world is the wing. And if there is someone on the wing who makes you feel something, that feeling becomes enormous. It fills the space. It is not like a relationship on the outside where you can go home, you can have space, you can let it breathe. In prison there is no breathing room. The relationship is everything, because everything is the relationship. And when it ends – and they usually end, badly, in that confined space – it ends in front of everyone.

'I had quite a bit of trouble just from not being interested,' she said. 'If you're not interested, it causes problems. You can see how people go along with things because they're scared, and then suddenly they've got a sort of protection, or a girlfriend, or whatever it's called in there. Women who would never even consider it on the outside. Every two or three women, one of them is in something like that while they're inside.' The relationships between officers and prisoners were equally visible to those paying attention. 'There were relationships between officers and prisoners as well,' she said. 'I knew a lifer who had something going on with a female officer. The officer left her job over it. They thought they were going to get married. They didn't, in the end. But she left the job. It was real, as mad as it was. If there was an officer and a prisoner, you could tell. You'd see them slide letters under the door. You'd see them staying in the office together too long. We're not thick.'

The formation of these relationships was not always mutual or freely chosen. The acute vulnerability of a new arrival – young, frightened, without social capital, unable to read the wing's existing alliances – made her a target for the kind of attention that could present itself as care while serving a different purpose.

Neah described an experience from early in her sentence with the precision of someone who had subsequently understood it fully. 'There was an older woman who took an interest in me,' she told us. 'Looking back, I understand what she was doing. At the time I didn't. She was very kind, very attentive. She brought me things. She looked out for me. She made me feel safe in a place where I didn't feel safe. And I was grateful. And then one day she made it clear what she wanted in return. And I . . . I understood then what all the kindness had been for. The penny dropped. And I thought: I know what this is. I know this. This is what they do on the outside, and I didn't recognise it in here because I wasn't looking for it in here.' She had ended it, she said, cleanly and without drama. 'But I was luckier than some. Some of those girls didn't know what was happening until they were deep into it.'

Eleanor arrived at New Hall having heard about the phenomenon but not quite believed the reality of it. It found her within the first two weeks. 'This girl from one of the other wings had decided she wanted to get to know me. Very full-on. She used to follow me everywhere, sit at the end of the table, come to my cell in the morning. She was really nice, actually – funny, good company. But after a couple of weeks, when she realised I wasn't interested, she was on to the next. Very much the same pattern every time. There are women in there with five kids back home who are very firmly someone's bird by the second week. You understand it – the institution, the boredom, the need for something. But it catches people out who aren't expecting it.'

Eleanor had navigated a different but related experience on her second stint at New Hall. 'She'd appear whenever I was in association,' Eleanor told us. 'Sit near me. Then next to me. Then she was always finding reasons to be close, to touch my arm, to sit very close at a table. It went on for about two weeks. I had to be very clear with her. I said: "I'm not interested, I'm not going to be interested, and I would prefer you to stop." And she accepted it. But it took that directness. You couldn't just ignore it and hope it went away, because in that environment it doesn't go away. It intensifies.'

Anastasia described the social architecture of these relationships at Drake Hall with a specificity that made clear how openly they operated within the community of the wing. 'When the bus pulled up at Drake Hall, there were lesbians waiting at the gate,' she told us. 'They would come and introduce themselves. Welcome you. Size you up. It was quite upfront, actually. There was no pretence about it. You were a new arrival and they were interested in whether you were available. At Drake Hall with its more relaxed regime, these things were more visible than in a closed prison. They were just out there.'

Nicola described the complications that arose when

relationships broke down in the closed environment of New Hall, with nowhere for either party to go and everyone else watching. 'We had two women who had been in a relationship for a long time – years, going back through multiple sentences,' she told us. 'And a new arrival came, who one of them became interested in. And it destabilised everything immediately. The jealousy, the accusations, the manipulation of everyone around them. The whole wing got drawn into it. It affected association, it affected work, it affected healthcare because one of them stopped eating. These are real relationships with real emotional stakes, and when they go wrong in an environment where you cannot leave and cannot escape the person you are no longer with – it is very hard to manage.'

The question of transgender prisoners in the women's estate has been one of the most contested policy areas in the Prison Service in the past decade, and it was one that several of our contributors had managed.

Suzy described cases she had encountered across her career with a care for the complexity that the public debate often lacks. 'I had a transgender prisoner who was predatory,' she told us. 'She had had top surgery but not bottom surgery. She was placed in the women's estate. And some of the women were frightened of her. Not because of who she was but because of what she did. Her behaviour was predatory. And the difficulty was separating those two things – what she was and what she did – in an environment where the women she was housed with couldn't easily make that separation, and where their fear was real, regardless of what produced it. A lot of staff, including me, had never come across this before. I had to say to my head of security, I need you to research this, have someone else in the office while you do it, but I don't want it in my browser history.'

The policy context was one she found inadequate to the complexity of the cases it was meant to govern. 'The guidance is not nuanced enough,' she told us. 'There are transgender women in the estate who pose no risk to anyone and who are themselves vulnerable. There are transgender women who do pose a risk. The question of how you distinguish between them, and what you do with that distinction in practice, is much more difficult than any policy document acknowledges. And in a women's prison, where the population already contains some of the most damaged and vulnerable people in the country, getting that wrong has serious consequences.'

She drew a distinction between different directions of transition and how each had presented in practice. 'I think it was less complex, psychologically, going from female to male than the other direction,' she said. 'I've met a few female to male in women's prisons who were clearly transitioning, still in a women's prison while they finished their sentence. I think now they would go into a men's prison. But actually, there are so many young women who are quite boyish that they didn't stand out particularly. I do remember one who was going through hormone treatment, had a beard, very pleasant, just quietly wanted to get their sentence done. Two issues: very popular with the women on the wing, as you can imagine, a nice-looking man on a women's wing. And my security concern, because we had a lot of building contractors on site. I kept thinking, if that person queues up with the builders as they're leaving, my staff are not going to pick them out.'

Her longest view on the subject was in many ways the most striking. 'Back in the eighties and nineties, I think there were people who had transitioned or were clearly transgender and we just accepted them where they were,' she said. 'There wasn't a political issue. I remember somebody coming through reception in the women's prison and when you pulled the paper records, the back three were from male prisons, and then from female prisons, and you saw the point at which they'd had surgery. And nobody really blinked. It was just one of those things. And then lots of very boyish young women, whether because they were gay or because they were going to need to transition at some point, we just accepted that they looked like a boy and behaved like a boy. It wasn't a political issue like it is now. It's strange that when something becomes much more common, it gets more controversial rather than less, rather than normalised. Very strange.'

She also recalled a prisoner at Dartmoor from earlier in her career who occupied a different point on the same spectrum, and who was remembered with a kind of affectionate bemusement rather than the institutional complication that later cases would bring. 'When I was at Dartmoor, we had a guy,' she told us, 'and you know, he was always a bit of a joke, because – do you remember chinagraph pens, that you wrote on a whiteboard and then you rubbed it out? He was always stealing the chinagraph pens because he wanted to use them as eyeliner and stuff, because they always came in red and blue. And he was always – I don't think he was ever going to transition. He was just a cross-dresser, and he liked wearing make-up. Well, that is also a thing. And actually, it was always taken in really good spirits. It was just, you know, somebody going, it's the bloody chinagraph again. That guy – well, it was always a bit of a laugh. You just accepted people for what they were.'

Nicola had worked with a prisoner at New Hall whose gender journey over the course of a long sentence had been particularly difficult to manage institutionally. 'There was another one that was a male prisoner that was at Wakefield, that went to London and had a change to female,' she said. 'Came to New Hall and was on the segregation unit, then regressed back to being a male, called John again, but then decided to behave and become a female again. I found that a bit hard the first time I came across it, because the anatomy had been changed. That was the first one that I came across. Didn't look feminine in any shape or form, really. She got quite aggressive at times, but she's still got the manly strength. So John had gone through that whole process physically and then regretted it, but then reverted again, and I think ended up marrying a female in the prison. She was in for life.'

She also described a second case that had arisen in reception, requiring an immediate decision. 'We had a guy that had had his top half changed in Thailand, but he'd still got his todger, and he was in New Hall,' Nicola said. 'The governor said to me, "oh, there's a female coming from Doncaster courts, but we're not sure if she's had the operation." So I got a healthcare support worker to examine this person. I said to the staff, "get this person off the bus first. We need to examine them." It turns out that she'd not had the surgery. It was a male and we took her to Armley.'

She reflected on how the legal landscape had been shifting around all of this even as she was working. 'The understanding is that you get an easier time if you're a female than a male in a male jail, you know, or if they identify as a female but they're physically still a male, then they've got to go to the appropriate jail,' she said. 'Well, it was when I was working there, but it was starting to change. You know, the legislation around gender and passports and what you identify with. I mean, now, obviously you've got learning difficulties, autistic people, we always had them, but not as much. They get themselves into trouble a lot more, don't they? We understand that a lot more. But also, you've got the pronoun issue, haven't you?'

Suzy also addressed female sex off-ending, a subject that attracts less public attention than male sex offending but is more prevalent in the women's estate than is generally acknowledged. 'Power, not aggression, is usually the driver with female sex offenders,' she told us. 'It is not the same as male sex offending in its profile or its motivation. Women who sexually offend tend to be in a position of care or authority. They use that position. It is almost always about control. And the victims are almost always people over whom they have that control – children in their care, vulnerable adults they are responsible for. The Beverley Allitts and the Lucy Letbys and the Vanessa Georges. They are all in that category, though the specific acts are very different.'

'Male sex offending is often about power in a directly aggressive way,' she said. 'Female sex offending is a more complex psychological thing. There is still a power differential, clearly, between a teacher and a pupil, but it doesn't feel as overtly violent or aggressive. Female sex offending often involves supporting male abusers. The number of women who will acknowledge that their husbands or partners were abusing children, and either facilitate it or fail to expose it, is significant. I've met women who held a child down while the man abused them. Taking that secondary role. And I think that's why there's sometimes a different response to female sex offenders in prison. Women in there relate it to their own children and they get angry about it, and rightly so. But they don't quite operate the same hierarchical punishment system that men do.'

She described a case that illustrated the legal complexity of female sex offending, recalling a woman who was charged with assault by penetration, which is the female equivalent of rape under English law in terms of sentencing. 'People are surprised by that. They think rape is something that only men can do. But the law is clear and the reality is clear. Women can and do commit rape. The cases are less common. The profile is different. But they exist, and the women's estate holds them.'

Simon had encountered female sex offenders at Holloway across his career and described what set them apart within the population. 'They are treated very differently by the other prisoners,' he told us. 'In the male estate, sex offenders are the lowest of the low in the hierarchy. In the women's estate it is more complicated. A woman convicted of a sexual offence against a child – she is in serious danger from the other women. A woman convicted of something that involved another adult and some ambiguity – she may be managed differently. The hierarchy in women's prisons is not identical to the male hierarchy, but the deep antipathy to those who harm children is universal.'

One of the least discussed features of the women's estate is what happens to sex offenders once they arrive.

Wendy, who had governed prisons in England, Scotland and Australia and inspected the entire Scottish women's estate, was direct about what this meant in practice. 'Female sex offenders aren't put on a separate wing the way they are in the male estate,' she said. 'It does happen in the male estate too, it's just not as prevalent. I've known a fair number of fairly serious sex offenders, even paedophiles, who insist on going into the general population and who are well known in the community and have no trouble whatsoever. And I've known a few who happen to be lawyers who simply set up a legal practice, and it protects them. In the women's estate, it's just not as managed.'

Prisoners who spoke to us about their experiences described a kind of enforced tolerance. One woman, who had transferred from a closed prison to an open establishment, found herself sharing a wing with a significant number of women convicted of serious sexual offences. She was told explicitly that any confrontational behaviour towards them would result in her being returned to closed conditions immediately. The message was understood by everyone. The result was a strange social peace, fragile and coerced, in which women whose crimes bore no resemblance to one another were expected to live together without incident.

This compression of the population – the putting of everyone together because there are too few women to do otherwise – generates an intimacy that the male estate does not replicate. It generates conflict, yes, but it also generates something else: connection, dependency, tenderness and sex. At Hydebank Wood in Belfast, the question of sexual activity between prisoners is impossible to separate from the question of the site's unusual architecture. Since 2004, the women's prison at Ash House has shared its grounds with the Young Offenders Centre housing young men aged 18 to 24. The separation between the two populations was always less absolute than the official account suggested. Ex-prisoners and sources familiar with the establishment told journalists over the years that young men from the YOC were able to spend time with women from Ash House alone and unsupervised during periods when oversight was less rigorous. The establishment acquired, among those who knew it, the nickname Ridebank: a touch of Belfast humour about the sexual permeability of the boundary between the two sites.

In 2016, the implications of that permeability became very public. A prisoner who was on remand awaiting trial got pregnant while in custody. She had formed a sexual relationship with a young man held at the Young Offenders Centre on the same site. The case prompted immediate scrutiny of how the two populations were being managed, and supervision arrangements were tightened significantly in its wake. More recent inspections noted improvement. But the episode confirmed what many inside the prison had already known: that where men and women are held in such proximity, within sight of one another, crossing paths in shared spaces, the management of sexual contact becomes a challenge that no amount of formal policy can fully resolve.

The context in Scotland is different, but some of the dynamics are not dissimilar. The introduction of the Community Custody Units, with their domestic architecture and their emphasis on independent living, brought with it new questions about the management of intimate relationships. The units are designed to feel like home, and homes are places where people are intimate with one another. Women in the CCUs can leave the building for work and community access. They cook together. They share sitting rooms in the evenings. The social conditions are, by design, closer to ordinary life than anything else in the custodial estate. Whether the rules governing those conditions have kept pace with the philosophy is another matter.

The question of contraception and provision for sexual health in the women's estate sits at the intersection of institutional honesty and institutional denial. The official position that consensual sex cannot occur in a custodial setting is contradicted by the evidence of the people we spoke to. The deeper issue behind all of this is that women in prison have, in large numbers, been subjected to serious sexual violence before they arrive. Rates of sexual abuse in the histories of women prisoners are substantially higher than in the general population.

The effect of incarceration on women who carry that history, and who are then placed in settings where their bodily autonomy is again subject to institutional control, where they are strip-searched, where they live in enforced proximity to others they have not chosen, is something the prison system has only recently begun to take seriously as a design question rather than simply an operational one. The question of sex in prison, and what it means for a population of women who have largely experienced sex as something done to them rather than chosen by them, goes to the heart of what custody is for and what it does.

As you can see, the sex life of the wing encompasses relationships of all kinds. For those who are pregnant when they arrive, or who give birth in custody, the circumstances are totally different.

CHAPTER 17

Mothers & Babies

'I saw one – she had to hand her baby over to her
family. She'd kept her baby for the first year and a
half, then had to give it away. I couldn't imagine one
of my children being taken away. Absolutely not.'
BEV BUTLER

More than 60 per cent of women in prison are mothers. The consequences of their imprisonment for their children are among the most serious and the least discussed aspects of the female estate. Research consistently shows that children separated from their mothers by custody suffer worse long-term outcomes: lower educational attainment, greater likelihood of contact with the criminal justice system, higher rates of mental health difficulties. The intergenerational consequences of locking up mothers are not incalculable. They have been calculated, repeatedly. The calculations have not yet translated into a system that treats this as a reason not to lock up mothers.

239

Of all the chapters in this book, this was the hardest for us to write. Even harder than the chapter on self-harm. Even though we can see all the goodness and compassion being built deeper into the system all the time.

Approximately 6 per cent of women entering prison in England and Wales are pregnant. More than 17,000 children a year are separated from their mothers by imprisonment. These are not marginal facts about a marginal population, they are the central, undisputed and consistently under-acknowledged reality of what the women's custodial estate does and who it does it to.

The Corston Report of 2007, commissioned by the government following the deaths of six women at HMP Styal in a period of 12 months, recommended that custodial sentences for women should be reserved for those who commit serious and violent offences and pose a genuine public risk, and that investment in community alternatives was urgently needed. It was the most comprehensive review of women's imprisonment in modern British history. Its headline recommendations were not implemented. The women's population has continued to be dominated by those convicted of non-violent offences, many of them primary carers, many of them with histories of abuse and mental ill-health that predated their offending. Their children have continued to bear a consequence that the system records under nobody's name.

The mother and baby units that exist within a small number of women's prisons represent a genuine attempt to preserve one of the most important relationships in a child's early life. They are also, by definition, places where infants are raised behind bars. The fact that MBUs exist at all reflects something compassionate in the system. The fact that the system makes them necessary at all reflects something that compassion alone cannot resolve.

There are currently seven mother and baby units in women's prisons in England. Each has a limited number of places. Each requires a formal application, assessed by a board that weighs the interests of the baby against the security requirements of the institution and the suitability of the mother. Places are not guaranteed and can be lost. For women who secure a place, the MBU represents the only means of keeping their child with them during their sentence. For women who do not – or whose sentence does not allow for it, or who give birth before a place becomes available – the separation is immediate and absolute.

Bev Butler was among the first officers at New Hall when it transitioned to a women's prison and described the mother and baby unit in its early years. 'Oh, yeah, they built a mother and baby unit not long after we'd opened. I think that was probably one of the things that went alongside with the segregation unit. I can't remember how many were actually in it – eight to ten rooms. And they were gated off, you know; other inmates couldn't go in there. So yeah. But some were already heavily pregnant. And then they were due to give birth but they could keep the babies for a year and a half, and then they would have to hand them over if they were still in there; they would have to hand them over. One lifer did that. She had to hand her baby over to her family. She kept her baby for the first year and a half, and then had to give it away. Obviously, they came to visit with the baby, but what else? I couldn't imagine one of mine being taken away. Absolutely not. Would that have been for adoption or for a foster period or something? Yeah, depending on what sentence they've got. Yeah. And what they wanted as well. Social services would get involved with some inmates that had probably had children taken from them before, because they were on drugs and things. They would go into foster care. We'd take them to the hospital, they'd give birth, and then social services took over.'

Kay, who also worked at New Hall, described the unit in practical terms. 'The baby unit was only small. It held nine. Four cells, but they were never locked and a twin room if anyone had twins. A lot of those women got pregnant to try and not have a prison sentence. Females are the nucleus of a family; they are the home runners. When females come into prison, they still want to run the home.'

Juli recalled a sight from the New Hall grounds that stayed with her. 'There was a road inside New Hall. I'd gone for a walk around so they could have the babies outside. There were about six with pushchairs side by side. Visually striking. Think of the long term if your child is born in prison.'

One case on the unit had stayed with her in a way that the others had not. 'We had a woman who was quite clearly from a different background from most of the women on the unit,' she told us. 'Well spoken. Well educated. Her parents were mortified but she had got into bad company. She had been in a relationship with someone who had gradually introduced her to heroin. Groomed her, really. By the time she was arrested she was six months pregnant. She hadn't even known she was pregnant. She had been in such a state for so long that she had stopped tracking her own body. She arrived on the MBU still barely able to take in what had happened to her life. And there was her baby, arriving into all of that.' We reflected on this, because you cannot look at a case like that and feel that the system has got it right. This woman needed treatment and support and community. She got prison.

Juli had spent years working alongside the mother and baby unit at New Hall and described the tensions it generated around media access. 'We had a film crew come in to film the MBU,' she told us. 'And I refused to let them film the babies. In three or four years' time, when you're going to school and taking that child to the nursery or to primary – what if these things they're filming are then replayed later on, and the other people in that school, the other mothers, see this and know who you are, and whispers go around, and your child is then known as being born in a prison? There was a significant argument about it. I held firm, and the babies weren't filmed.'

Yvonne's account of giving birth in custody, and of the months that followed, is one of the most moving in this book. She arrived at Styal seven months pregnant, and her first impressions of the place set the tone for everything that came after.

'When I came into Styal, it felt like a concentration camp. You have got the long huts, the aerial view of it, you know the kind of buildings I mean. And you have got the VP wing and you have got the open houses as well, and the mother and baby unit. On my first night, the first thing I thought was, I have got to hold it together. I was pregnant. It was December.'

The admission process, and the strip search that was part of it, she described in Chapter 4. The pregnancy made it especially humiliating and horrendous.

Yvonne's account of the mother and baby unit at HMP Peterborough is in that chapter too, where the context of her arrival there is fully established. What belongs here is what came before it: the months at HMP Styal, seven months pregnant, in the weeks after her arrival in December, during which the conditions for keeping her children close were not what any policy document might have prepared her for.

'It's one hour a day exercise,' she told us. 'And if you have prams, they won't let you out. So I never left that room with those kids. It was that corridor. That is all you have. You literally had the corridor and the kitchen. One hour of exercise a day and if your baby has a pram you cannot go. So your world is a corridor. And your babies are in that world with you, and you cannot take them outside, and you cannot let them run, and there is nowhere to go. That was Styal. That was the mother and baby unit at Styal.'

She described looking at the other women on the unit

and understanding that for some of them, this was not the worst version of their lives. That was perhaps the most disturbing thing, she told us. Not that the conditions were bad. That some of the women were grateful for them.

She described one of the women she encountered in those early weeks, whose situation illuminated the broader senselessness of who ends up inside. 'There was a woman in there who was Polish. She had been pushed into dealing drugs by her mother to pay off a debt. She had tried to pass whatever it was and she was just pulled for it. She had done nothing wrong. And you are putting her in there, in a worse situation than the one she came from. There is no sense in that.'

The healthcare she received during her pregnancy was something she returned to with strong emotion. 'They told me there was a measurement on the back of the baby's neck that suggested a possible problem. They told me this and then made me wait four weeks for a proper scan. Four weeks, sitting with that. Everyone else going to hospital appointments with their partners. I was completely on my own. Completely isolating. Then when I was near my due date they still were not moving quickly enough, not taking it seriously. I was nearly overdue. I knew I was going into labour. They made me wait. When Jadine finally arrived, at least some of the officers who were there that night were decent. They kept me talking, they looked after me. But I should not have been going through any of that in there in the first place.'

She was clear that the experience was not uniformly

bleak, and that one officer made a difference that was hard to overstate. 'There were also some really decent officers. And for me, personally, if it were not for Jo, I honestly do not know how I would have come through. Jo would literally come to the door and say, "get your arse up, you are going to eat." She kept me going, she was incredible.'

The postnatal depression that followed Jadine's birth was something Yvonne managed alone, concealing it from the people around her because the stakes of disclosure felt too high. 'I had postnatal depression. I did not let it show because I was being watched and I did not want them to take Jadine. I just held it together as best I could. Even when I had Junior, I cried every day. Every single day. I believe that the trauma I went through during that pregnancy affected him. When babies are born to mothers going through severe trauma, it can affect the child's development and DNA. Junior had difficulties that I trace back to that. It is a poorly researched area but I can well believe it.'

Giving birth in custody is, for some women, not a possibility to be managed but an event that occurs without adequate preparation. Tragically, stillbirths have occurred. What this represents is a systemic, traumatic and fatal failure.

Nicola remembered an awful case with the bleakest possible outcome within the MBU system: a woman who gave birth and was not allocated a place. 'I had a prisoner who gave birth and the baby was taken from her immediately,' she told us. 'There was no MBU place available.

The baby went straight into care. She was back on the wing within days. And you just – you look at her and you think: how does a person come back from that? How do you come back to a wing full of people and a routine and roll calls and lock-up, when days ago you gave birth and then your baby was taken? She didn't speak for a week. And then she started going through the day again, and you watched her, and you thought: the system has done something to this person that is going to last the rest of her life. And there is no mechanism for acknowledging it or addressing it. She just has to carry it.'

Nicola also noted that some of the hardest cases she witnessed involved babies who never made it on to a mother and baby unit at all. 'Yeah, well, they did have mother and baby units. Where they can come in, in the risk assessment, they can stay on the mother and baby unit till the child is a certain age. Some of them were actually taken in hospital, away at birth, because they were considered the same risk. I've got a younger brother. I don't know where he is. My mum, with a mental health instability, had a fourth child, and that child was taken away at birth. So sometimes the social workers were involved all the way along, because that child was under care even before it was born.'

Debbie worked on the New Hall mother and baby unit for approximately two years. Her account of it is both unsentimental and fond. 'I worked on there for a couple of years actually. I'm not at all maternal. I haven't got any children, and I'm not really maternal but I actually really enjoyed working on there. It was a small unit. I think it held nine. When it was full it wasn't an overly big unit. Some of the girls on there had got pregnant because they thought they'd be avoiding a sentence, and that rarely worked.'

'It was a nice environment. We used to take them for walks around the prison, and we had nurses on duty: two nursing members of staff on duty. We used to take them for walks around the prison route. And there was like a television room. They had to stay in the cells, but it wasn't like a normal cell. It was a nice environment. And the babies stayed until eighteen months, and then they had to be handed out.'

Bev had seen a handover at New Hall that stayed with her. 'I saw one,' she said. 'She had to hand her baby over to her family. She'd kept her baby for the first year and a half, then had to give it away. And obviously they came to visit with the baby, but what else, you know? I couldn't imagine one of my children being taken away. Absolutely not.'

That image of a woman who had spent eighteen months feeding, holding and learning a child, then standing in a prison reception room and passing the child into someone else's arms is one both the institution and the mother can be forced to accept. The arrangement is, in its way, the system at its most humane: the baby is going to family, not to strangers, and there will be visits. But the moment of physical separation is the moment of physical separation, and what the woman walks back to afterwards is a cell.

The children who are not on the MBU – the older ones, the ones already at school, the ones in the care of grandparents or foster families or simply managing without – are the population that the system most consistently fails to account for. Yvonne earlier described the consequences for her own older children with the candour of someone who had spent years understanding them.

The day of her release was not, as she described it, a moment of relief. 'On the day I was released I had a double pushchair, all my stuff loaded on to it, two babies, and nobody came to collect me. My mum was at the salon. She has had her own difficulties. I was not angry at her. But I just walked out with that pushchair, on my own, and that was it. That was coming home. When I got on the train I sat in my seat and it was just so silent. I was not used to silence. Women's prisons are incredibly noisy. The medication bell would go off at the same time every day and everyone would rush for it. You are walking down the corridor and you are just filtering through the noise constantly. And then suddenly you are on a train and there is quiet. I could not get used to it.'

Work is being done to effect positive change. The MBU at HMP Peterborough has a playroom. It has its own kitchen, with highchairs and all the facilities needed to support mothers in feeding their kids. Cells have private bathrooms and the doors are not locked. That said, it's a privilege to be in there, and there are so many hoops to jump through that it is often under-occupied. As we have seen, many mothers will also choose for their babies not to be in prison with them no matter how caring, safe and comfortable the facilities are.

The invisible consequence of women's imprisonment – the children who are not counted, not supported, not followed into the years after the sentence ends – is perhaps the clearest argument the system provides for its own inadequacy. The cost of it is not paid by the prison. It is paid by the children, and by the communities they grow up in, and by the prisons they themselves, in too many cases, eventually enter.

The blood that is spilled in a women's prison is not only the blood of violence. It is the blood of lives that have been reached by the institution in ways nobody planned and nobody counted. That is the subject of the next chapter.

CHAPTER 18

Blood

*'I remember one lady, she stabbed her boyfriend in the arm
while they were drunk, and he died from that one stab.'*
BEV BUTLER

The stories that bring women to prison are not usually
stories about violence committed freely and for gain.
They are stories about violence absorbed, over years, until
the point of absorption was reached. They are stories
about the relationship between what happened to a woman
and what she eventually did, and about a justice system that
tends to locate those two things in separate categories –
victim and offender – when the reality places them on a
single, continuous line.

Domestic violence is a disturbingly huge feature of
what drags women into the criminal justice system. Many
of those whose crimes involve violence committed them
in the context of abusive relationships, either against the
person who was abusing them or because of the conditions
that abuse created. Understanding this does not provide a

legal defence, but it is essential context for understanding who is in women's prisons and why.

Suzy's decades of professional observation granted her some extraordinary insights.

'If you went round a women's prison and asked how they got there, you would get the same story nine times out of ten,' she told us. 'Started shoplifting. Got into drugs. In an abusive relationship. And here we are. I call her Miss Prisoner. She is in every women's prison in the country. She has been there as long as there have been women's prisons. Her details change. Her postcode changes. Her age changes. But the shape of her story does not. And we have never, as a system, found a way to interrupt that story before it reaches the gate.'

Suzy's typical female prisoner had a journey into custody with a horrible logic to it. 'Imagine the journey of a woman who's been convicted of continual theft and shoplifting. This is an absolute generalisation, a composite Miss Prisoner. She's thieving because she has a drug habit. She has a drug or alcohol addiction because the only way to cope with life in the environment she's in is to blot it out with substance misuse. So go back. Why is she feeling the need to blot out reality? Most often it's because they live in abusive relationships. They've been abused since a very young age. They start taking substances as a way of coping. The substance addiction leads to the crime, leads to that grinding revolving door.'

The drug dependency that features in so many of those stories was something she had come to understand differently after her own experience with strong pain relief following an operation. What she described was one of the most psychologically penetrating observations we've ever heard.

'I had a morphine drip after an operation,' she told us. 'And for 11 hours I just wept. I could not stop. I did not know why. And afterwards someone told me that is what morphine does – it releases whatever you have been suppressing. The pain barrier that you maintain just goes, and everything you have been holding comes out. And I thought: that is why women self-medicate. That is what the heroin is doing. It is not about the high. It is not about the pleasure. It is about the 11 hours of weeping. It is about the release of everything that there has been no safe place to put. And when I understood that, I understood the women I was governing in a completely different way.'

One ghastly case that had stayed with Bev was a woman at New Hall whose boyfriend had been murdered at her instigation, his body afterwards dismembered and disposed of in pieces. The crime that put her in prison was not the killing itself but what flowed from it — the conspiracy, the disposal, the role she had played in arranging what happened that night.

'She was really nice,' Bev told us. 'Her boyfriend was a really big lad and she was terrified of him. He was narcissistic and obsessive. She decided she didn't want to be with him any more, and the only way she could get rid of him was to have him murdered. She let somebody in one night, and what they did was stab him. The blade broke in his neck. He put up a big struggle as he was a big lad. They hacked him and cut him up and spread his body around. It was sad. I mean, I know it wasn't a nice death for him, but even the police said they were pleased he was gone, because he'd caused that much trouble. When she told us all the things he'd done to her, you couldn't help but feel sorry for her.'

The phrase 'the only way she could get rid of him' sits at the heart of how women like this end up in the women's estate. There is a man whose existence has been the organising fact of the woman's life for years before the offence. There are, almost always, other ways out that someone with more resources, less fear, a better lawyer or a less violent partner might have taken. The court records the killing. The evidence of what produced it sits, where it tends to sit in these cases, somewhere off the page.

Bev described two further cases that captured how routinely alcohol and the home featured in the women she received at New Hall. Neither was the kind of crime that made the papers. Both were the kind that filled the wing.

'Then there was another one, an older lady, in her sixties,' she said. 'Her and her husband were both alcoholics. She went into the kitchen, took out a knife, stabbed him. And sometimes it was only one stab. I remember one other lady, she stabbed her boyfriend in the arm while they were drunk, and he died from that one stab. It was mainly domestic, yes. Definitely. And alcohol involved, yes.'

A single stab. That was the distance, in many of these cases, between a difficult marriage and a life sentence. The proximity of the kitchen knife. The drink taken. The argument that had taken some shape on this particular night for reasons that would be picked over in court without ever quite being settled. Bev's two sentences contained the mechanics of a significant proportion of the women's estate.

Nicola described two cases that illustrated contrasting routes to serious violence in the context of relationships defined by abuse and control. 'There was one case that stands out. She had killed her husband and they exhumed his body, and she'd been slowly killing him with arsenic. There was another lady whose partner had kept her locked up in the cellar, got her addicted to heroin, and then when she came out, basically attacked him because she was withdrawing. He smacked his head on a table and died. So she was done for manslaughter. There's all different reasons, you know. But I would say there is a lot that are drug-related, yeah, or domestic abuse, or narcissistic abuse, that's massive, isn't it, increasing.'

Suzy described the specific way that violence by women is perceived differently in court and in wider society, and where she believed a partial shift had begun.

'Violence, if a woman goes up in front of a judge, it's such an anathema, particularly to your old white male judges, that women are violent. It almost doubles in its being abhorrent because it's not what society expects women to do. If a man gets in a pub fight and starts blowing up, you know, that's what they do, and they'll have a fight and move on. If a woman decides to smash a bottle and put it in somebody's face, it's, "oh my God, women don't behave like that. She's clearly off the scale."

'I think there was a bit of a shift when there was a cultural move into laddish behaviour and women in gangs. But I think there's another shift now, perhaps since Rotherham, where women in gangs are beginning to be seen as having been the victim to be in the gang in the first place. They haven't made a conscious decision to be laddish like a bloke. They're driven, some of them, by survival. Or groomed into it. Which a young man can be as well. That's what's happening with a lot of the county lines gangs, with very young kids being drawn in.'

Suzy told us about a striking case from her time as a governor, when the crime's wider context was important. 'I remember one woman, a farmer's wife. Her husband had been conducting affairs for years, psychological abuse, taunting her with it. He was going out that evening with one of his women, and she picked up the shotgun and said, "if you leave the house, I'm going to shoot you." He walked out of the house and she shot him in the backside. And most of us, well, you couldn't say it officially, but most of us thought, good on her. She was very quickly in an open prison, didn't serve very long, was a lovely woman. Just driven to a point. No threat to society. Not going to go around shooting anybody else. There is an argument she should have just walked away from the marriage, but that's not that easy for some people, is it? She served her time without any trouble whatsoever.'

Yvonne was direct about her own route to custody, and about her perception of the specific mechanics of how the system processes women who act in self-defence. 'I was attacked with a bottle,' she told us. 'I acted in self-defence. That is what happened. But when the police came, I was the one who was arrested. Because I was the one who was left standing. And that is often how it goes with women. The one who is left standing is the one who goes to prison.' The investigation of what led to that moment – who had been doing what to whom, over what period of time – is a much more complicated thing to establish than the fact that a person is standing there and another person is on the floor, though, of course, we also note this is recounted from Yvonne's perspective.

She described what happened on the night of the incident that led to her conviction with the clarity of someone who had gone over it many times and still could not fully make sense of the outcome. 'When the incident happened, I was seven months pregnant. She went for me first with a bottle, to my head. And I stood there afterwards, waiting for the police. I had been attacked. I needed to tell them. When the police came, I thought they would see it straight away. That this was never a section 18. I was so adamant about that. Maybe if I had accepted the section 18, things would have gone differently. But I thought, anyone with eyes can see that this is never a section 18. There were no cameras and it was a dark little club. It was my word against hers. Someone did come forward but she had her own history and that counted against her.'

Vanessa described what it was like to manage women whose crimes had involved children, and offered a longer view of how attitudes within the system had shifted. 'Many years ago, female prisoners were considered mad not bad as it was inconceivable that women could cause such damaging crimes. Some people even today think that, and many female prisoners are taken to mental asylums instead of prison because, how can a woman whose job it is to nurture and care for children end up murdering them? If you did, you must be mad. But you can't ignore that there are bad female prisoners.'

Suzy described how notorious prisoners manage status in the women's estate, and how that dynamic differs from the male equivalent. 'Women manage status differently to men. Men need a hierarchy. It's really useful for a group of men to have someone at the bottom of the pack, because it means everybody else is above them. I'm not sure women need to have that person to look down on in the same way. They do get angry and upset if someone's in for crimes against children and they've got children outside. They can relate to it and they get angered by it. But they don't quite need that hierarchical structure in the same way that men do.

'A notorious prisoner coming in gives women a different kind of status opportunity. If you've got your face in the newspapers and everyone knows your name, that's one way of being at the top of the pecking order in a women's prison.

Female lifers carry a kind of awe with them because people think, she must have done something terrible and she's got over it, she knows her way around. They know all the staff; they know how to work the system. The long-termers are actually often quite useful for the short-sentence women. They need somebody to look up to, someone who knows the ropes and can help them navigate it.'

Not all of the women in prison for violent offences have the same story. There are women who commit violence for reasons that have nothing to do with self-preservation or accumulated despair. The justice system must hold both kinds. What the testimony of our contributors suggests is that it has been much better at holding the second kind than understanding the first.

For some of the women who pass through the prison estate, the damage they carry is not only the damage of the offence and its consequences. It is the damage of mental illness, of addiction, of a life that the system of criminal justice was never equipped to address. That is the subject of the next chapter.

CHAPTER 19

Mental Health, Self-Harm & Asylum

*'She said: "When I die, I hope I'm in prison,
because at least someone will care." And that's
the lives these women lead.'*
SUZY DYMOND-WHITE

Walk into any women's prison and the scale of the mental health crisis becomes apparent almost immediately.

According to the Prison Reform Trust's Bromley Briefings, 82 per cent of women in prison report having mental health problems, compared with just over half of men. The rate of self-harm in women's prisons runs at more than eight times the rate in men's prisons. In the 12 months to September 2024, there were 21,412 self-harm incidents recorded in the female estate alone, a rate of 5,906 per 1,000 prisoners. HM Inspectorate of Prisons, in its 2024 thematic review, described the situation in stark terms: some of the most acutely unwell women in the country are being held in prison simply because there is nowhere else for them to go.

Between the prison estate and the secure psychiatric hospital estate lies a deadly gap. The women who fall into it are among the most damaged and least visible people in the criminal justice system: too mentally unwell to be safely and humanely managed in a prison, not sufficiently unwell to meet the threshold for secure hospital transfer or meeting the threshold but unable to access a bed because there are not enough of them. Women with serious mental illnesses are significantly overrepresented in the prison population relative to the general population. The overwhelming majority of those women will never be transferred to a secure hospital. They will serve their sentences in a setting that is not designed to treat them, managed by staff who are not trained to treat them, with access to clinical support that is insufficient for the level of need they present.

The physical realities of managing this crisis fall to a relatively small number of healthcare staff working under considerable pressure. Bev recalled one woman on the wing whose compulsive swallowing presented an almost-daily challenge. 'We had one lady on there with obvious mental health issues,' she said. 'She was a swallower. So if she got hold of anything, she'd swallow it. Toothbrushes, pens, combs, knives, forks, anything. We had to give her a paper plate, and then another paper plate cut off for a spoon, because she was that bad. Before that we'd given her her meals with a plastic plate and a plastic knife and fork. One day all we got back was a plate and a fork. "Where's your knife?" "I've swallowed it. So we sent her over to the nurses and they ordered her to go to hospital. They X-rayed her and had a look down her throat. They said, "we can't see anything." They had another look. "Oh yeah, we can just see the end of it." Her stomach was scarred horrendously where it had been opened up so many times. One time she swallowed a toothbrush and they just said, "she'll have to pass it." They wouldn't operate. Did that put her off? No. She carried on.'

Nicola, a mental health nurse who worked for many years at New Hall, arrived knowing almost nothing about what she was walking into. 'When I first went I was like, oh my God, what am I doing here?' she said. 'Then it's not for everybody. People would come and think, now it's too enclosed, but nobody attacked me. I was supported very well by the prison staff, and it's listening to people and understanding the reason why you're told to do something.'

What Nicola quickly came to understand was that the healthcare wing served as a kind of triage point for the prison as a whole, housing not just the medically unwell but everyone whose risk level or volatility made ordinary wing life impossible. Over time, even the shared bays that once allowed lower-risk women to be housed together were replaced by single cells. 'There was a hospital wing,' she said. 'And on the hospital wing, we used to have bays of four, so the risk-assessed patients. Over the years, it became where every cell was a single cell, because the problems were so bad or they were risk assessed not to be sharing. And it's same on the wings. They risk assess women to see if they're fit enough, stable enough, to share with somebody. And on the healthcare, that's what happened.'

One of the most significant complications in attempting to assess and treat women on arrival was the extent to which mental illness and substance dependency were intertwined. For many women coming through the gate, it was impossible to separate the two. 'When I was doing mental health assessments, a lot of them were actually detoxing off alcohol or detoxing off drugs,' Nicola said. 'And you can't do mental health assessments on those sorts of people. So keeping those people safe when they're rattling or unwell, because if you look at it, it's like the chicken and the egg. Did the mental health problem start first, or are they self-medicating a mental health problem? It's very difficult as a mental health person in a prison to work out what that initial issue is, but at the end of the day, we've got to keep that person safe.'

The conditions in which women arrived at a prison's reception area made early assessment extraordinarily difficult. Nicola described the experience of seeing someone for the first time with no history, no documentation and no continuity with whatever care they may have been receiving in the outside world. 'You're looking at them as a whole person, aren't you?' she said. 'You would see them in reception. That's where we first see patients. They come from court. They could be sentenced to a week, a month, remanded for God knows how long. They're presented to us with no history. Because, again, the medical information that we get for these people is very minimal. We don't link to the outside world. So that person is presented in front of you with, you know, looking emaciated, with God knows what sentence they've got, and you've suddenly got to keep that person safe and make an assessment to see where they're going to be allocated in the prison for the next few weeks.'

The problem of arriving with nothing was not merely administrative. 'Nobody comes with anything,' she said. 'Nobody's got chips, you know, like your doctor's surgery. Yeah, I could work in a doctor's surgery, and a patient comes in and all I've got is what's on the computer in front of me. Whereas when they come in from the courts, they could be coming from anywhere in the country or the world, and they're presented in front of you. So what medical information do you get from them? Luckily, if somebody is known to the courts, you might get a little bit or probation or whatever, but very rarely do you, especially when they land on you at past seven at night.'

In the most serious cases, the healthcare wing effectively functioned as an improvised psychiatric unit. But there was a fundamental and legally significant limit to what could be done there. Unlike a hospital operating under the Mental Health Act, a prison could not compel a patient to take medication or receive treatment against her will. 'A lot of the time would be containing women with acute psychiatric problems that there were no beds for in the community,' Nicola said. The risk lay in the fact they were not under the Mental Health Act, so they could not actively treat women against their will, whereas in a hospital, you would do because of the section and you can treat them. In a prison they don't have that same jurisdiction. Nicola's sadness was clear as she recalled constantly seeing women who are acutely poorly and as a mental health nurse, just containing people, did not always feel ethically and morally right.

Under the Mental Health Act 1983, a prisoner who requires inpatient psychiatric treatment must be transferred to a secure hospital bed. In theory, this should happen within 28 days of that need being identified. In practice, it routinely did not. An HM Inspectorate of Prisons thematic review published in 2024 found that only 15 per cent of prisoners requiring transfer were moved within the recommended 28-day time frame. The average wait was 85 days. In some cases, it exceeded a year.

During that wait, nursing staff had to manage women whose psychosis might make them violent, delusional and unable or unwilling to engage with any form of care. Nicola described how a relatively straightforward unlock could become a carefully coordinated operation, where staff count themselves lucky if prisoners take their medication. You can't force them to take medication. You prepare for a situation. You can't section them. If we know somebody's volatile, then you would have officers there ready to potentially restrain that person. Yeah, we wouldn't just unlock that cell and let somebody who's unwell out. It'd be controlled, a controlled unlock. There'd be people there that would need to be there. And unfortunately, if they become violent or aggressive or whatever, then they would have to be restrained and put back in. We couldn't medicate them against their will. We're not sectioning in prison.'

Psychiatric support, when it existed at all, tended to be provided through visiting clinicians rather than permanent on-site staff. 'A doctor. You know, we've got a psychiatrist, but the psychiatrists are not on site every day. They come and visit and do clinics,' Nicola noted. Between those visits, the responsibility for managing the most acutely unwell women fell to nurses and prison officers who might have no specialist training in forensic mental health.

Nicola described a particular young woman who arrived having been moved from prison to prison, spending most of her time in her cell, refusing food and refusing contact. 'There was one girl that came and she just kept moving around prisons.' As we knew, this is what happens when prisoners become a problem or their behaviour changes. As a nurse, Nicola was full of compassion for this girl, and keen to treat and reassure her. That isn't always possible, though. 'She wouldn't talk to staff. Eventually she slashed her arm and required 95 stitches. She was put on the seg.'

What Nicola described was a pattern that repeated itself across the female estate. Women were moved when they became unmanageable, which disrupted whatever fragile trust or stability they had built. The disruption itself tended to make things worse. They were moved again. The system generated its own momentum.

She also described the lottery of finding a bed when

a transfer was finally needed. 'It depends on, it's like with if you broke your leg in your local hospital, how long would you wait to get on the ward and have an operation? Yeah, depends which hospital you go to. How many patients run the ward. So there's no set answer. It depends where that person lives. If they originate from Mansfield, you would think that they will try and get them to Nottingham, but they might have to go to Scotland for a bed. And it depends on what the problem is with that person. Somebody who's got severe personality disorder or psychosis would have to go to a certain facility. Soon as they hit the prison setting, it already throws up medium secure, doesn't it? So you can't admit them to a normal mental health hospital. It's got to be a secure environment, because they've already been through the judicial system.'

Nicola described how the volume and the regularity of self-harm incidents changed the way staff experienced them, and the ethical difficulties that created. 'Yeah, yeah, it's tough,' she said. 'And obviously we're called to people that have tried to hang themselves and cut their wrists and swallowed stuff. And you know, it's a daily occurrence. And for some people, it's too much. You don't become uncaring about it. It just becomes another incident. Yeah, which is wrong, but it's the way that you deal with it. If you talk to a lot of people that work in trauma, you become desensitised to it, but you know, from a mental health point of view, if somebody is self-harming and injuring themselves, they're obviously troubled, but they're not ready to talk. So until they stop doing whatever they're doing to get the relief, then you can't talk to that person. It's hard sometimes, and the officers have limitations on what they're able or willing to do as well, so it can be quite difficult.'

She also described the way in which suicide watch had become, for some prisoners, a mechanism rather than a safety measure. 'The inmates who learn to know what to say: if they say, "I'm going to kill myself and hang myself," then those words automatically put them on a watch, don't they?' she said. 'Yeah. And then the kick-off. I didn't want to be on this watch. I didn't mean it. Well, you've said it now. We've got to follow it up. And it seems to be a bit of a manipulation thing sometimes, because the ones that really are troubled and they're going to do something are quiet. They're not the ones that are going to shout about it. So it does produce a lot of work for the officers and nurses to sit down and do these reviews. But the problem is, you're getting a lot more troubled, complex drug people in. You're going to have these issues, aren't you?'

Simon described two gut-wrenching and tragic in-stances of self-harm.

They were both cutters. The first 'had cut a vein in her arm,' he told us. 'And she had taken a biro tube and she had inserted it into the cut to regulate the blood flow. She was using the tube to keep herself in a state of controlled bleeding. Not dying. Not stopping. Just bleeding, at a rate she could manage through the tube. The precision of it was extraordinary. The planning. The level of anatomical understanding required. And what it told you about the depth of the pain she was in and the level of control she needed over that pain. She was not trying to die. She was trying to manage an internal state that was otherwise unmanageable, and she had found a method. A terrible method. But a method.' One lunchtime the staff came to find him because she had been in the toilet for a very long time. 'We went in and the pool of blood was unbelievable,' he told us. 'We managed to save her.'

The second was a woman who 'self-harmed deliberately and methodically as a form of stress management,' he told us. 'She was very articulate about it. She said: "when the pressure gets to a certain level, I cut. And then it releases. And I can function again." She wasn't in a crisis when she did it, she was managing. And the cutting was the management tool. Not a cry for help. Not an attempt on her life. A coping mechanism. And the question you are left with is: what level of distress do you have to have lived with, for how long, before that is the coping mechanism you arrive at? What was done to this woman, and for how long, and by whom? We used to give her a safe place to do it,' he told us. 'She would self-manage the self-harm. She had all the medical supplies, the staff would ensure she had everything she needed, and she would cut the vein, bleed, stop it herself, Steri-Strip herself, and then she would be fine. That release was what she needed to get through the next patch,' he said. 'We were not encouraging it. We were managing something that was going to happen regardless, and doing it in a way that kept her alive.'

He was clear about what the prison could and could not offer these women. 'We could keep them safe in the moment,' he said. 'We could cut them down, we could get healthcare there, we could put them in a safer cell, we could put them on constant watch. What we could not do was address what was underneath it. The prison is not a therapeutic environment. It cannot be. And so the women cycle. They self-harm, they are treated, they self-harm again. And the staff who manage it carry that with them. You cut someone down and they are alive. And the next day you cut them down again. And you ask yourself: at what point does this become something other than care?'

The most extreme case Juli Flintoff encountered at New Hall – the 19-year-old woman who had grown up with dogs, who was kept behind a Perspex door, who ended on life support as Juli prayed at her bedside – is described in an earlier chapter. Here, it need only be named. What it represented was the failure of every institution that had touched that life before the prison received it.

Anastasia had been on the landing at New Hall when a woman she knew self-harmed severely because of spice use, having been visibly deteriorating for days beforehand. 'She slit her own throat,' she told us. 'From taking spice. Literally across the landing from me. She had been self-harming for days before that. Everyone could see it. It was not a secret. It was not something that was missed. It was observed, every day, and nothing happened. And I keep coming back to that. Why did no one help her?

She was right there. The evidence was right there. And she got to that point before anyone intervened. And I ask myself: if I had said something different, done something different, would it have changed anything? And I don't know the answer.'

Yvonne described a case at HMP Styal that represented the specific failure of the system at its most consequential: a woman who died when she had two days left on her sentence. 'She had two days left on her sentence,' Yvonne told us. 'Two days. She had asthma. And she couldn't breathe. And her inhaler was being treated as a controlled item – as contraband, essentially. And she died. With two days left on her sentence. And her parents came. And the officers wouldn't speak to them. They closed the door. They couldn't face it. And I understand that they couldn't face it. But her parents were there, and their daughter was dead, and no one would speak to them.'

She reflected on what that case represented. 'It is not that people don't care,' she said. 'Some of the officers in these places care enormously. But the system does not create the conditions for that care to be effective. It creates the conditions for things to fall through the gaps. And the gaps are filled with people. Real people. And when they die in the gaps, someone has to go and speak to their parents. And sometimes they can't.'

Neah described the therapy offered during her decade in the estate with a precision that exposed the gap between what was provided and what was needed. 'They offer you therapy in prison,' she told us. 'And sometimes it is real and sometimes it isn't. And you learn to tell the difference. Because the real work – the work that gets somewhere – makes you worse before it makes you better. It has to. And the system doesn't want you to get worse. If you get worse, that's a problem for the wing. So mostly what you get is the kind of therapy that gets you through the day without incident. Which is not the same thing as getting better. It is the thing that looks like getting better while nothing changes.'

She had encountered one psychologist across her sentence whom she described as genuine. 'She was the only one I trusted,' Neah told us. 'Because she told me the truth. She told me that some of what I was going to have to deal with I was going to have to deal with myself, after I got out, in the world, with actual support. Not in a session once a fortnight in a room with a camera above the door. That was the most honest thing anyone in that system ever said to me, and it helped. More than any of the sessions.'

She also described what it had felt like to beg to be returned to prison, and what that said about the alternative. 'I begged them to put me back inside, once,' she said. 'I'd come out on tag and I had really bad anxiety and overthinking spiralling into the worst place. What if I'd accidentally hurt someone? I was in a really bad moment. I kept going to the police station begging them to put me back in. When they finally did and that door shut behind me, I had never felt peace like that in my whole life. No one could get to me. Nothing could happen. That was quite something, that feeling, and it is really sad.'

The Assessment, Care in Custody and Teamwork framework – ACCT – is the mechanism by which the Prison Service is supposed to identify and manage those at risk of self-harm or suicide. An ACCT document is opened when a concern is raised, reviewed regularly by a multi-disciplinary team, and closed when the risk is assessed as having reduced. The framework is not nothing. Its consistent implementation is another matter. What the evidence from our contributors describes is a system in which the paperwork of care and the reality of care are frequently not the same thing: in which an ACCT can be open, reviewed and closed around a woman whose distress is as visible as Anastasia described on that New Hall landing, and nothing changes.

The excellent Samaritans' Listener scheme – in which trained prisoner volunteers provide confidential emotional support to their peers – operates in most women's prisons and is consistently evaluated as one of the most effective provisions in the estate. It works because the woman is talking to another person who has been where she is. That is, for many women in the estate, the most therapeutic thing available to them. That it works so well is a tribute to the people who deliver it. That it is needed so desperately is an indictment of everything around it.

There is a broader policy question about why so many acutely unwell women end up in prison at all. The Corston Report, published in 2007 following the deaths of six women in HMP Styal in a 12-month period, recommended a fundamental rethinking of the way the state responded to women who came into contact with the criminal justice system. It called for community-based alternatives, for wrap-around support that addressed the complex and interconnected factors driving female offending.

Suzy shared her argument with us about institutional provision that she had come to over many years of working in the system. 'We should also, as a society, accept that there are people for whom institutional life is what they need and what they can cope with. Some people have a very simple outlook on life and what they like is being told when to get up, being taken to breakfast, being structured through a day. There used to be institutions. I think we need a 21st-century version of a place where people who genuinely cannot cope with the outside world can live, where the expectation isn't that we're going to put you through a degree and you're going to go out and buy a house. Just somewhere that provides routine and safety and community for people who need exactly that.'

Transfer from prison to secure hospital operates under the Mental Health Act 1983. A prisoner who is serving a sentence and who develops a mental disorder of a nature or degree that warrants detention in hospital for treatment can be transferred under Section 47, which requires the approval of two registered medical practitioners and the Secretary of State for Justice. A restriction direction under Section 49 is usually added, meaning that the patient cannot be discharged or granted leave without the Secretary of State's consent. These legal provisions exist. The gap between their existence and their consistent application is where the problem lies.

Simon had encountered at HMP Holloway a prisoner whose circumstances illustrated what the failure of timely transfer looked like at its most extreme. 'There was a prisoner sent to Holloway who had poured petrol on themselves and set fire to themselves,' he told us. 'As a result of the fire, they had lost their breasts, their ears, significant portions of their face. They were in the process of gender reassignment and they were living in the women's estate. And they were at Holloway. In a prison. In that condition. And you think – what is this person doing in a prison? What treatment can a prison provide for someone in this situation? What does it mean for this person to be managed by wing staff who are not clinicians, in a building that was not designed for them, among a population that does not know what to do with what it is seeing?' He paused. 'You do the best you can. You always do the best you can. But the best you can is not what this person needed.'

The cost of the mental health crisis was borne, every day, by the women inside and by the staff who cared for them. Nicola's account of her working life was not one of despair, but it was shot through with the frustration of someone who understood what could be done and what was actually available. 'In some ways, I do miss the camaraderie and the support and the little bit that hopefully I did help some of those women that came through the system,' she said. 'But I think my empathy just, it was tested to the limit, and you can only do that sort of job and give so much for so long, you know.'

Suzy, reflecting on 38 years in the service, gave the most succinct summary of what the crisis meant in human terms. She had known one woman for 30 years, from when she was a young offender of 17. 'She used to chat to me like we'd grown up together, because in her mind, I'd known her on and off for over 30 years,' Suzy said. 'She died recently, I understand. I remember her once saying to me that her health was deteriorating. "When I die, I hope I'm in prison, because at least someone will care." And that's the lives these women lead.'

The mental health crisis in women's prisons is not a condition at the margins of the estate. It is its defining characteristic. Open prisons represent something different: the point at which the system attempts, for those who have served long enough to reach them, to move in the other direction.

CHAPTER 20

Open Prisons, Rehabilitation & the World Outside

'If you're not going to make some noise for the people who can't be heard, then what was it for?'
NEAH TUOHY

The distance between a closed women's prison and an open one is not just a matter of security classification. It is the distance between a life defined entirely by institutional constraint and a life in which the beginning of a return to the world outside is made possible. For the women who make it to an open establishment, the transition can feel almost unreal after years in closed conditions.

The testimony of those who have experienced it is often some of the most hopeful material in this book.

HMP Askham Grange is one of only two open prisons for women in England and Wales. It is situated near York in a Victorian house built in 1886 as a private country residence and has been a women's prison since 1947.

Prisoners are usually transferred to Askham Grange having already served three years or more at a closed establishment and can remain for up to three years to complete the final part of their sentence. The focus is resettlement. Mary Bell served the final part of her sentence at Askham Grange before her release in 1980.

Askham Grange is set in the stunning village of Askham Richard. The road outside has cutesy signs warning of ducks crossing. There is a lovely and very popular cafe, The Grange, as well as a gift shop and nursery selling seasonal plants. There is barely space to park outside with the crowds on a sunny day. It's staffed by charming prisoners who uniformly wish you a happy day as they cash up cupcakes and bedding plants. It feels like a success story.

HMP East Sutton Park is the second of England's two open prisons for women. It occupies a Grade II listed manor house in Kent and opened as the first ever open borstal for girls in 1946. It holds approximately 100 prisoners, mainly women serving life sentences or long determinate terms who are approaching release, many working outside the prison in paid employment. HM Inspectorate of Prisons described East Sutton Park in 2016 as exemplifying what a good women's prison should be.

It is set in beautiful grounds with picnic benches outside and friendly sheep running towards visitors from the surrounding fields. With a gym in the outbuildings to the right, the drive sweeps up towards a grand entrance hall. The farm shop at the back isn't easy to find, but is a real gem when you do. As we have mentioned earlier in the book, our contributor Suzy remembered it with great affection as her first real posting, with greenhouses, farms, and women going out to work.

The contrast between the relative humanity of the open estate and the relentless pressure of closed and remand prisons runs through most of the accounts this book contains. East Sutton Park and Pucklechurch, in Suzy's telling, are almost separate countries. The same job, the same system, the same women. The difference is the regime, the architecture, the assumptions baked into each place about what the person inside it is worth and what she might become.

Tracy Mackness established her sausage business after serving five and a half years of a ten-year prison sentence for conspiracy to supply cannabis. Her path into criminality was one she described without self-pity, as the predictable consequence of limited options and limited horizons. 'Working on the stall was all I wanted to do and I left school with no qualifications,' she said. 'I thought I wouldn't have to learn anything other than the stall and I had to start doing other things to earn money. That led me into a life of crime, petty crime, doing things I shouldn't be doing to earn money and then, as the years progressed, I got into bigger things.'

Tracy's time at East Sutton Park open prison in Kent changed the direction of her life entirely. She began working at the prison's pig farm and fell in love with a Saddleback pig named Biddy, took an NVQ in pig husbandry, and subsequently completed a college sausage-making course and an apprenticeship at a butcher's before establishing her company. 'I could not believe there were no locked doors,' she told us. 'You walk in and there are no locked doors. You can go outside. And they need looking after every day, whether you feel like it or not. And I thought: I can do this. I can be responsible for something. That was the thing. Not the pigs specifically. The responsibility. Having something that depended on me turning up.'

The Giggly Pig Company grew from 30 Saddleback pigs purchased from the prison to a business producing over 65 different sausage flavours. 'I worried about what I would do when I got out of prison,' she said. 'I was never going to go back to the life I had; it wasn't an option. I never expected Giggly Pigs to work but it went crazy and I have a product people really want to buy.

'People talk about rehabilitation like it's a complicated thing,' she told us. 'But it's not. It's actually very simple. You give someone something to do that is real, something to learn that they can use, something to be responsible for. And then you trust them. And most of the time – not all of the time, but most of the time – they rise to it. Because people want to be worth trusting. That is the default. It has to be worked against. The prison system spends a lot of its time working against it, and then wonders why the outcomes are what they are.'

Not every open prison experience is Tracy's. The open estate varies as much as the closed estate in what it offers and how it is run, and the gap between its ambition and its delivery can be significant.

Yvonne served the final part of her sentence at HMP Askham Grange in North Yorkshire. Her account of it is measured and specific. 'Askham Grange is an open prison,' she said. 'It was much softer. You had a room, not a cell, no bars. Your door was not locked. You could move around. After what had gone before, it almost felt unreal. You could go out to work and come back. It was much better. At Askham Grange you also get more interaction and a bit more structure. There was work. I did not work at Styal or Peterborough because of the babies, so I had just been sitting there all day, which was unbearable. But even at Askham Grange, the work pays almost nothing. A pound a day putting sponges in boxes.' She was clear that the ambition of the open estate and the economic reality of what it offered were some distance apart. 'This is supposed to be the part of your sentence where you prepare for the world outside. And you are making sponges for a pound a day. You're supposed to be developing skills, building confidence, practising normal life.' From Yvonne's account, the economic reality of what you're doing is so far from normal life that the preparation is largely theoretical.

The moment the gate opens is the moment the system's investment in the individual is most visibly tested. What is on the other side of the gate – accommodation, support, employment, continuity of healthcare, a probation relationship that functions – determines whether the work done inside translates into anything lasting. The evidence from our contributors is consistent: for most women, what is on the other side of the gate is not adequate to the need.

When the gates opened for the last time, Yvonne described what happened in direct terms about the inadequacy of what the system offered at that point. 'When you come out, there is virtually no aftercare,' she said. 'You can try and access something through the NHS but there is nothing properly in place. You are just set loose. That is what it is. And of course, if you have come from a chaotic situation, a violent relationship, a drug habit, you are going straight back into exactly the same environment, because nothing on the outside has changed while you were inside. The short sentences make it worse. There is not enough time for rehabilitation, not enough time for anything on the outside to shift. You go back into the same situation and the cycle starts again. I met women who said there was almost a relief in going back inside, because at least it was away from the chaos they were returning to. That tells you everything.'

The stigma that followed women out of prison was another form of sentence that the system imposed without acknowledging. Yvonne described its weight in personal terms. 'The stigma is the biggest challenge after you come out,' she said. 'My dad died and I was not able to go to the funeral. I did not tell people where I had been. I was carrying the whole thing on my own. The stigma follows you.'

The practical mechanics of rebuilding after a sentence are formidable for almost everyone who leaves custody. For those with convictions for serious offences, the disclosure requirement is an obstacle that sits between the sentence and any realistic prospect of stable employment. Dainya described the difficulty of disclosure, and how she eventually found a way through it. 'I struggled getting employment, and then that knocked me down a bit, because you've got a criminal record, so certain jobs, it's like, okay, I can't apply for that job,' she said. 'And then anything that has disclosure in it really limits me. I'm thinking, what would I do? They're going to ask me about my criminal record, and I literally didn't know how to disclose it. Then I found Working Chance through a friend, and being spoken to about disclosures kind of made me have to look into myself a little bit and accept that actually, you've been where you've been, but it's okay. You've just got to know how to disclose yourself. There are ways of doing it, words that you can use. And the more I was practising my disclosure, I was like, okay, this is becoming a bit easier. It's almost like doing affirmations.'

The experience had crystallised a larger purpose. 'I want to use that page to advocate, and then down the line I would love to start a programme aimed at young teenagers about grooming, because it kind of is in alignment with my whole reason behind ending up in prison and my early teenage years,' she said. 'Like I said, doing this journey does make me revisit stuff, and I've come to realise that sometimes you go through some trauma and you kind of bury things at the back of your brain. Every time that I speak my story, something new pops up and I'm like, oh my gosh, I forgot about that. I think sometimes when you're going through intense trauma, you don't realise other traumas are happening too.'

The turning point had come for Dainya, she told us, when her first son was about two years old. 'I just got to a point of being in, I was just there, thinking, and just felt like I was going around in circles. I'd just kind of hit a point in my life, like, oh, my God, I'm getting older, or what am I doing with myself? Something's got to give, 'cause I just felt lost.' She had tried Bible study, she said, and it helped to a point, but the employment difficulties continued to knock her back. When a cousin recommended a free Zoom mindset call, she had been sceptical. 'I had an ego of, like, I know everything, there's nothing anybody in this world can tell me that I don't know.' But she tuned in, found the mentor authentic and relatable, and eventually joined a mentoring community where women from different walks of life shared their stories. The mentor pushed her out on to social media in ways that were uncomfortable at first. 'She made me do things that I would never think to do, just literally took me out of my comfort zone with social media, and speaking my story. I still struggle with it a little bit, but with practice, I know I'll get better.'

It was through that process that an organisation noticed her posts and reached out, eventually leading to an invitation to share her testimony at a Black History event at HMYOI Isis. 'That was probably really emotional,' she reflected. 'I'm like, do I want to do this? I'll shed a tear, but I didn't let them see because I was thinking, oh my gosh,

I can't be crying in front of everybody. But I just took a moment for myself and then – again, these people have the same experiences as me. I realised maybe this is my calling.' From there she was connected to the Safety Box and its organiser Nathaniel, she told us, who invited her to work on the Aspire Higher programme – delivered to schools, prisons, probation, and to probation officers and police. Her drug sector role had also taken her back inside, she said, including into Belmarsh. 'Seeing life through the other side. Emotional, emotional sometimes because it brings you back to that sensitive part of being on the other side and incarcerated.' She reflected that it was only in adult life, and as a parent, that the full shape of her early years had become visible to her. 'I just feel like somewhere along the line, my purpose is to shed light on awareness of certain experiences that I've had.'

Nicola described what happened for the younger women, those going back to the circumstances that had produced the offending in the first place. 'It varied because it depends on the social setting,' she said. 'Some of the youngsters were referred back to young offending units and probation officers, and some of them were going back to the family that had created the problem in the first place. You know, when they're homeless, they'd have to just turn up to the homeless department and have nothing. They'd have the clothes that were on their back, a bit of money in their pocket, jump on a train and be expected to start life again. What are you going to do? You're going to go back to what you know, aren't you?'

Eleanor Brown was initially resistant to the psychology provision at Askham Grange. She came to view it differently. 'I've always been one of those people who says, get on with it. We all have hard times. So when I got referred to psychology, I was like, I'm not doing that. I don't need help. Nobody's making me. And after about three sessions – I did about 25 weeks with her in the end – she started asking me questions that just changed my perspective. I went through a break-up while I was inside, and I worked with her through it. She asked questions I would never have asked myself. About boundaries, and what I'd accepted, and what had happened to me that I'd just normalised. I'd never have recognised any of it before. It started as something to do through the week, and turned into actually, this is really helpful. But there's no magic wand. You either let it go and move on, or you use it. That's all there is.'

Neah Tuohy reflected on what ten years of her life had made her, and what she had done with it. 'I've got more life experience in prison than I have outside,' she said. 'Ten years in there, four years out here. It's mad, because it's a completely different world, and it's really crazy trying to navigate the flip. You have to adapt entirely to one way of life in prison and then you get out and you have to do it all over again out here. Some people go back because their brain is just wired to what they know. That is their home. And they've become institutionalised. But I was obsessed with getting out. That was all I thought about. The last sentence I thought that was the end. But now, working with young people and drawing on what I know, I think you've got all this experience and understanding of things that other people out here don't have. And if you're not going to make some noise for the people who can't be heard, then what was it for? The majority of the women I'm still friends with from inside are doing the same. Running companies, doing youth work, advocacy. You've got to try and do something with it. Otherwise it's been a bit of a waste.'

For those who navigate release without crisis, what follows is not straightforwardly freedom. It is the work of reconstructing a self that has been compressed and managed and suppressed for the duration of a sentence. Neah described what that reconstruction looked like from the inside. 'I spent so long suppressing who I was in there that when I came out I didn't know who I was,' she told us. 'You learn to make yourself small in prison. You learn not to take up space, not to attract attention, not to be the one who stands out. It is a survival skill. It keeps you safe. But you do it for long enough and it becomes you. And then you're outside and you're supposed to be yourself and take up space and have opinions and make choices. And you don't know how. You've forgotten how. Or you never properly knew, because you went in at an age when you were still figuring it out. And then you were doing something else entirely for the best years of that process.'

Yvonne, speaking about what she hoped to build from her experience, expressed what she described as the only reason to believe the experience was worth enduring. 'My absolute dream would still be to open somewhere where women can get proper therapy, parenting classes, drug support, a framework for getting out of the cycle they are stuck in,' she said. 'A lot of women in there are in complete chaos and have never been given any kind of structure. They need something around them to show them what life could look like if it were framed differently. I went through all of that for a reason. I have to believe that. If I can do something for one person, it is worth it.'

Suzy was characteristically crisp and intelligent about what the evidence says and what the system does with it. 'Everything we know about what works for women in the criminal justice system says: small, community-based, trauma-informed, with continuity of relationships,' she told us. 'The women respond better to smaller settings. The evidence for this is not contested. It has not been contested for decades. Baroness Corston said it in 2007. The research has said it consistently ever since. And yet we maintain a women's prison estate that is built around large institutions, long distances from communities, with high turnover of staff and minimal continuity of care. We know what works, we just don't do it.'

On the specific geography of the estate she had spent her career in, she was blunt. 'If you close Eastwood Park – which you should, because it is the wrong kind of provision in the wrong kind of building – the nearest prison for women in the west of England is in Derbyshire,' she told us. 'That is the estate we have built over 150 years.

And we maintain it not because it is right but because closing anything is politically and logistically difficult. We are prisoners of the estate as much as the women are.'

She was equally direct about what had been lost. 'We lost a lot of good stuff,' she said. 'It's all about cutting costs. We all know women respond much better to smaller, community-style settings. But it's not cost-effective to run small units. Is it cost-effective to have people coming back again and again and not achieving anything?'

Anastasia's description of leaving prison was moving and surreal. 'Mum and Dad were both waiting for me,' she told us. 'I gave all my stuff away, though, so I literally just walked out in what I was wearing. I left all of my stuff with the girls in the prison. Mum was going to buy me a new whole wardrobe. So I was just like, you know what, I didn't want to wear anything that I wore in there ever again. It just reminded me of that place.'

The return itself felt almost impossible to process. 'It doesn't actually feel like you've ever been,' she said. 'Suddenly it all feels like a dream. Like, it never happened. Yeah, it's just completely, you just don't feel like you've ever been there and it just feels like a dream because it's just so different to real life. It's just like, I felt like I wasn't even there. So I got back in the car with my mum and dad. I was just like, this is going back to normal. It's not like you've never been; it's just crazy how it all changed. It's like a different dimension, I'd say.'

She reflected on what it had left in her. 'I still think about it on a daily basis. If you've been to jail, I don't think you ever forget, especially when it's something that's taken you out of your comfort zone and something that you've never been around in your life and people like that, I don't think you'd ever forget. If you know what I mean. Like, you see why people get stuck in the jail routine, they keep going back. You can see why people do that, but obviously I've just been lucky that I have the support that I have. I've never got into trouble again, really. Yeah. I think it was more like Stockholm syndrome, that's what it is. And I'm lucky that I never got into that sort of frame of mind. I fell into this in the first place to end up going to jail because obviously I was just listening to older lads and I wasn't listening to my mum. My mum was telling me something, hanging around with them – you don't listen to your mum and dad at that age, do you? No, exactly. I regret it now, but you can't change the past, can you?'

The women in this chapter are not exceptions. They are what becomes possible when the system allows it.

CHAPTER 21

Conclusion: The Future of Women's Imprisonment

*'I've heard some right horror stories, but that's what
people don't realise. All the outsiders and the general public
don't see half of or understand half of what really goes on.
They don't know what's behind it all. They think, oh, they
committed a crime, they deserve to be locked up and the
key thrown away. But everyone's got a story.'*
TRACY MACKNESS

This book, like all our *Inside* books, has attempted to
bear witness to a world that most people in Britain pass
through life without ever encountering. The women inside,
the officers who manage them, the nurses who treat them,
the governors who carry responsibility for all of it: each of
them inhabits an institution that operates largely beyond
public sight, surfacing in the national conversation only when
something goes catastrophically wrong, or when a name like
Rose West or Lucy Letby brings the cameras to the gate.

What emerges from meeting and listening to the people

who work in these places, and to the women who have passed through them, is not a simple story. It is not a story about monsters, though some of the women described in these pages committed acts of extraordinary violence and cruelty. It is not a story about incompetent or uncaring institutions either, although the institutions are often stretched far beyond any reasonable capacity. It is a story about a system that was designed primarily for men, built around assumptions about male offending, male risk and male need, and that has never been adequately remade for the women it also holds.

As of December 2024, around 3,600 women were held in custody in England and Wales, a figure some 8 per cent higher than it was in April 2021. More than three quarters of them have been convicted of non-violent offences. More than half are serving sentences of less than six months. Sentences too short for any meaningful rehabilitative work to take place, but long enough to cost a woman her housing, her children, her employment and whatever fragile stability she had built.

The consequences of that failure are measured in numbers that should disturb anyone who reads them. Self-harm in women's prisons runs at more than eight times the rate in men's. In the 12 months to September 2024, there were more than 21,000 recorded incidents of self-harm in the female estate alone, and 41 per cent of women who have died in custody since 2014 died by their own hand, compared with 28 per cent of men. The women who come through reception with no medical records, presenting to a nurse late at night with no history and no continuity of care, who may be detoxing, may be acutely psychotic, or may be in the early stages of pregnancy.

The officers and nurses who manage this, day after day, deserve fuller acknowledgement. Bev Butler, who spent her career at New Hall, developed ways of managing the unmanageable: adaptive, practical responses to situations no training could fully prepare you for, from paper plates to prevent swallowing to the careful, patient negotiation of a controlled unlock with a woman who had not spoken in a week. Nicola, working as a mental health nurse in an institution that had no legal power to treat the most acutely ill women in its care, sat outside a cell every morning at ten o'clock for three weeks, not because she was required to, but because she understood that consistency was the only thing she had to offer. These are not extraordinary people in the sense of being exceptional. They are people doing a job that most of us will never see, carrying a weight of responsibility that most of us will never experience or understand.

The cases that attract the widest public attention, the women whose names appear in headlines and true crime documentaries, represent something genuinely exceptional within the female prison population. Rose West, serving a whole-life tariff for crimes of almost incomprehensible sadism. Lucy Letby, whose murders of infants in her care produced a response of collective disbelief. Joanna Dennehy, who sought out men to kill. Myra Hindley, who became, over the decades of her imprisonment, a symbol for the entire question of whether punishment can ever truly be said to have been served. Beverley Allitt, Emma Tustin . . .

The fascination these cases generate is not difficult to understand. Female serial killers are statistically rare, and the rarity itself lends them a quality of the aberrant, the inexplicable. The offences that produce the most sustained coverage tend to involve a particular kind of violation: the nurse who harms those in her care, the mother who destroys the child she is supposed to protect. The horror, in these cases, is inseparable from the betrayal.

The women who make up most of the prison population are not Rose West, though. They are women who stole to feed an addiction, women who were present when a partner committed a crime, women who fought back against violence and were prosecuted for doing so, women whose mental illness was never diagnosed, women whose path from childhood trauma to the dock was as straight and as predictable as a line drawn on a map.

Scotland has taken a different path, at least in aspiration. The development of community custody units designed to keep women close to their families and communities, embedded in a wider policy framework that treats imprisonment as a last resort for women rather than a default response, offers a point of comparison that those seeking reform in England and Wales have repeatedly cited.

The revolving door that brings women back through the gate is not a mystery. Homelessness on release, the withdrawal of community support at the point of recall to custody, the impossibility of maintaining employment or family relationships across multiple short sentences, the recall of women to custody for technical breaches rather than new offences: all of these are known, documented and persistent.

Dainya Ebanks found the strength to break away from that potential cycle, as she movingly explained to us. She also has a very strong sense of what needs to be done:

On my low days, I just wanted to die. I hated the decisions I had made that landed me there. I blamed everyone but myself. When family dynamics changed, I blamed my absence and carried that weight heavily. Even now, it still comes back in moments.

But growth forced me to face something uncomfortable. I had to take accountability for my own actions.

At the same time, I had to learn that not everything was in my control. Understanding that difference has been one of the hardest parts of my journey, and it's something I'm still working on. Self-development isn't a phase – it's a lifestyle.

I had to dig deeper into why I made certain decisions, what patterns I was repeating, and how to break them. That meant being honest with myself in a way I hadn't been before.

It also meant learning to share my story.

At first, that wasn't easy. There was shame, fear, judgement. But I started to understand that my lived experience had value – not just for me, but for others walking a similar path.

That shift was strengthened through my spiritual journey too.

Coming to know God gave me grounding and purpose. It helped me see that what I went through wasn't the end – it was part of my development. Growth is continuous. A lifetime of learning, correction and self-awareness.

Resettlement after prison was not easy. I was excited to leave, but also nervous. My dad picked me up, and I remember feeling two things at once – relief and uncertainty. I was stepping back into a world that had moved on without me, including family dynamics that had changed and didn't feel better.

Within two weeks, things broke down at home and I had to move into a bail hostel. That was another adjustment, another environment to survive in. Freedom didn't mean everything was fixed – it meant learning to rebuild from scratch.

Today, I put all of that into action through my work.

I work with an organisation called The Safety Box, delivering gang intervention, knife crime awareness and self-defence programmes for women. I also help train probation officers and police, and I work directly with probation clients, schools and young people through workshops and summer programmes.

Alongside this, I advocate for women who have been through the criminal justice system through my brand, 'Thank God I Went to Prison'. It's about turning lived experience into empowerment – helping women rebuild without shame and find direction after prison.

I also serve as a board member for organisations supporting women into employment, training and education after custody, including Working Chance. That work matters deeply to me because I know what it feels like to come out and not know where you fit.

And there is still more I want to build – but I'm not ready to speak on everything yet.

What I will say is this – prison didn't break me.

It built perspective, accountability and purpose.

And my time in HMP Holloway was just the beginning of everything that came after.

What would change if the system were remade from first principles around the needs of women? A presumption against custody for women who are not a danger to others. Properly funded community alternatives, women's centres with stable long-term financing rather than the patchwork of short-term grants that has characterised provision since Corston. A healthcare system that can follow a woman from the community into custody and back out again, rather than starting from scratch at each transition. A sentencing framework that takes seriously the impact of imprisonment on children and families as a material consideration.

We came into this project as writers who had spent years listening. We left it as something closer to advocates – a word we do not use lightly. Advocacy is not the same as partisanship. It does not require us to look away from the violence, or the harm, or the cases in this book that defy any easy sympathy. It requires only that we insist on the full picture: that the woman behind the statistic had a life before she arrived, and will have one after, if the system allows it. Most of the time it does not. That is not inevitable. It is a choice.

A society that locks people up has an obligation to examine why, and what for, and whether the outcome justifies the cost. That cost is not only financial, though a prison place for a woman runs to more than £50,000 a year, against a few thousand for a place in a women's centre. It is the cost measured in the children separated from their mothers, in the women who leave custody more damaged than they arrived, in the staff who carry the weight of an impossible task without adequate support, in the deaths that should not have happened and the self-harm incidents that run, by the Ministry of Justice's own count, at one every few minutes across the estate.

The women who dominated the headlines, whose crimes were of a severity that places them in a category apart, will remain in custody for the rest of their lives, and rightly so. The system was built, in part, for them, but it was not built only for them. For everyone else, for the woman detained on remand who will never be convicted, for the woman serving six weeks for a debt she could not repay, for the woman whose mental illness was finally dealt with by sending her somewhere that cannot legally treat it, the question of whether any of this was necessary is one the system has been reluctant to ask of itself.

It is time it did.

Not everyone we approached felt they could reopen the doors they had closed on some dark chapters in their life. One particularly moving example, a former officer, recalled their work with young offenders who 'were such a heartbreaking, challenging, but sometimes rewarding group', but feared if she told us that 'every one of those instances will trace back to a troubled individual, some of whom took their own lives.' She concluded that 'unfortunately my service will have to stay buried within me. Even some of the remembering has given me more sleepless nights.'

We used the phrase 'sliding doors moment' a great deal when we were trying to describe this book. For every woman who deserves or needs to be incarcerated, there seem to be many more who would be better served somewhere else. Of course, this holds true for many male prisoners too, but so many of these women are one bad relationship or decision from where any of us could be. This isn't just a book, it's a call to arms, and it changed our lives writing it.

We have three children. We thought about them often while writing this. About what it would mean to be separated from them by a cell door, to hear a lock turn, to measure their growing up in visiting orders. About the women in this book who did exactly that, and who came through it – or did not. About Yvonne, who walked out of Askham Grange with a double pushchair and no one to collect her. About Neah, who spent ten years inside and four years out, and who asked the question we have not been able to stop thinking about since: if you're not going to make some noise for the people who can't be heard, then what was it for?

This book is our attempt at an answer.

Glossary of Female Prison Slang & Jargon

Prison language is a living thing. The terms below are drawn from the female estate in England and Wales and reflect the language used by prisoners, officers and healthcare staff across the establishments described in this book. Some are shared with the male estate; others are particular to women's prisons. A number have drifted into wider use; others tend to remain behind the walls.

A

Adjudication – The formal disciplinary hearing conducted by a governor when a prisoner has been put on report for a rule breach. Known informally as being nicked or going on the sheet.

Association – The period during which prisoners are unlocked from their cells and permitted to move freely within a wing or communal area, typically for a set number of hours each day. Association may be used for socialising, using the telephone, watching television or accessing wing facilities. Reduction or withdrawal of association is a standard disciplinary sanction.

Auntie – An older, established prisoner who takes younger or more vulnerable women under her wing, offering protection, guidance or simply company. The relationship can be genuinely maternal or quietly exploitative.

B

Bang up – To be locked in one's cell, or the act of locking prisoners in. Also used as a noun: bang-up is the period during which prisoners are confined to their cells, typically overnight and during certain hours of the day.

Basic – The lowest privilege level in the Incentives and Earned Privileges scheme, imposed as punishment. A prisoner on Basic has access only to the statutory minimum: a bed, bedding, one set of clothing and limited canteen.

Block, the – The segregation unit. To be sent to the block is to be placed in segregation, either as a punishment or for a prisoner's own protection. Also referred to as the seg or the digger.

Book One – The designation applied to a prisoner placed on the E-list. A Book One prisoner requires a named officer escort for any movement and that officer must obtain permission before any transfer. The cell is stripped of all but the most basic items overnight. Named for the formal register in which E-list prisoners are recorded.

Bumblebee suit – The yellow and green distinctive clothing worn by prisoners on the E-list, so called because of the colouring. Designed to make escape attempts immediately visible and to mark the prisoner clearly for all staff.

Burn – Tobacco, or a cigarette. One of the most significant currencies in the prison economy since the indoor smoking ban of 2007, which made it scarce and therefore more valuable.

C

Canteen – The prison shop from which prisoners purchase additional food, toiletries and permitted personal items using their private cash or wages earned from prison work. Also refers to the shopping itself: it's canteen day.

Canteen queen – An inmate who monopolises, controls or trades in commissary items, often using this as a means of exerting influence or power over other prisoners.

Closet chain – A length of chain with cuffs at each end used during high-risk escorts, allowing a prisoner to be restrained while maintaining some limited movement.

Controlled unlock – A managed and supervised cell opening procedure used for prisoners assessed as presenting a significant risk to staff or other prisoners. Rather than the standard unlock, a controlled unlock requires a minimum number of officers to be present, often in protective equipment, before the cell door is opened. Used routinely on healthcare wings and segregation units.

Crash pad – A cell used for taking drugs, typically by more than one prisoner.

Cut-up – The act of self-harm by cutting, most commonly to the arms. Also used as a noun: a cut-up is an incident of self-harm. To be found on a cut-up or to cut up is to have self-harmed in this way. One of the most frequent forms of self-harm in the women's estate and a persistent feature of life on healthcare wings across the female prison.

D

Detox wing – A dedicated wing, or section of the healthcare unit, for prisoners going through withdrawal from drugs or alcohol on arrival.

Dinosaurs – Slang, sometimes affectionate, sometimes derogatory, for older or long-serving members of staff who are resistant to change or, in some cases, no longer fully capable of responding to incidents.

Doing bird – Serving a prison sentence.

E

E-list – The escape list. A prisoner placed on the E-list has been assessed as presenting a significant escape risk. Placement triggers a specific set of security requirements including wearing the bumblebee suit, the Book One designation, cell-stripping overnight, and daily locks, bolts and bars checks. The consequences of placement are severe enough that most prisoners regard the E-list as a significant deterrent.

Enhanced – The highest level of the Incentives and Earned Privileges scheme, awarded to prisoners who have maintained good behaviour and engaged with their sentence plan. Enhanced prisoners receive additional privileges, including more time out of cell, greater canteen allowances, and in some establishments additional visits. Marked in some prisons by a red band worn on the wrist. See also Basic; Red band.

G

Gay for the stay – Colloquial term for the phenomenon of women forming sexual or romantic relationships in prison who would not do so outside custody.

Ghosting – Being transferred to another prison without warning, typically overnight and without the opportunity to inform family or legal representatives. Widely feared and used as a management tool for disruptive or high-profile prisoners.

Gov/Guvnor – A prison officer, or more specifically a governor grade member of staff. Used by prisoners and officers alike when addressing or referring to authority figures on the wing.

Grass – An inmate who informs on another prisoner to staff. One of the most serious social violations in the prison hierarchy. Also used as a verb: to grass someone up.

H

Hooch – Homemade alcohol, typically brewed illicitly in cells using fruit, bread, sugar and water fermented over several days. Neah Tuohy describes the method in considerable and hilariously expert detail.

I

IPP – Imprisonment for Public Protection. An indeterminate sentence introduced under the Criminal Justice Act 2003 and abolished in 2012, though those serving IPP sentences at the time of abolition continued to be held under the same terms. An IPP prisoner has no fixed release date and can only be released when the Parole Board is satisfied that the risk they present to the public is sufficiently reduced. Described by contributors as one of the most contested of all custodial sentences, producing a population of prisoners who have often served many years beyond the minimum tariff originally set.

J

Jail bent – Slang for a prisoner who adopts a same-sex relationship or identity in custody that they do not maintain on the outside. Related to gay for the stay.

Jailcraft – The instinctive, experience-derived ability to read the atmosphere of a wing, anticipate trouble, and manage people and situations in the specific environment of a prison.

K

Kite – A written note or letter passed secretly between prisoners, or occasionally between a prisoner and someone on the outside. Can also refer to a formal written request or application submitted to staff through official channels.

L

LBBs – Locks, bolts and bars. The daily security check routine in which an officer systematically inspects the physical fabric of a cell or area – locks, hinges, bars, window fixings, wall surfaces – to detect any attempt to weaken or compromise the structure. Required for all E-list prisoners and standard practice across segregation units.

M

MBU – Mother and baby unit. The dedicated residential unit within certain women's prisons where eligible mothers may live with their babies up to a specified age, typically 18 months. Places are limited and subject to assessment.

N

Nick – Prison. Also used to mean the police station or, colloquially, the act of being arrested.

Nonce – A prisoner convicted of a sexual offence, particularly one involving children. Occupies the lowest position in the prison hierarchy and is at serious and constant risk of violence from other inmates.

O

On licence – Released from custody subject to conditions set by the Parole Board or the Secretary of State, typically including requirements around residence, reporting to a probation officer, restrictions on contact with certain individuals, and prohibition on further offending. Breach of licence conditions results in recall to custody. The terms of licence can remain in force for the full length of the original sentence.

On remand – Held in custody while awaiting trial or sentence. Prisoners on remand are legally distinct from convicted prisoners and retain certain rights, including the right to wear their own clothing and to receive more visits. However, in practice, conditions on remand wings are often similar to or worse than those in the convicted population, and remand prisoners are held in establishments not always equipped for their needs.

On tag – Released from custody subject to an electronic monitoring curfew, typically requiring the wearer to be at a specified address during set hours. The tag is fitted to the ankle and monitored remotely. Used both as a condition of early release and as an alternative to custody for short sentences.

On the out – Life outside prison. References to family, relationships or circumstances on the out are a constant feature of prison conversation and correspondence.

P

Pad – A cell. Also used as a verb: to pad up with someone means to share a cell with them.

Phone cards – Prepaid telephone cards once used by prisoners to make calls from shared landline phones on the wing, and widely used as a currency in the prison economy before the introduction of in-cell telephones. Now largely obsolete in establishments where in-cell phones have been introduced.

Princess – An inmate who considers herself above the rules of the general population and expects preferential treatment from staff or fellow prisoners. Often used ironically by officers.

Put on report – To be formally charged with a disciplinary offence by a prison officer, leading to an adjudication.

Q

Queen bee – The dominant female inmate on a wing: the prisoner who controls the social order, mediates disputes and commands the loyalty of others. The role carries both status and risk.

R

Red band – A coloured band worn on the wrist by prisoners on Enhanced privilege status, indicating to staff that the wearer has earned additional freedoms and can be trusted with greater access and movement around the establishment. The colour and form of privilege markers varies between prisons. Used by Dainya Ebanks to describe her status at HMP Holloway, where it allowed her to request a single cell. See also Enhanced.

Restricted status – The classification applied to the highest-risk female prisoners in England and Wales, equivalent to Category A for men. Restricted status prisoners can only be held in designated closed establishments: HMP Low Newton, HMP New Hall and HMP Bronzefield.

S

Screw – A prison officer. Long-established slang, used freely by both prisoners and staff, though its origins as a derogatory term are not forgotten by all.

Seg – The segregation unit. See also Block, the

Spice – A synthetic cannabinoid, also known as mamba or black mamba, which has become the dominant illicit drug across the prison estate. Unlike cannabis it is difficult to detect through standard drug testing and can be applied to paper, letters or other flat surfaces, making it particularly hard to intercept at reception. Its effects are unpredictable and can be severe, including psychosis, unconsciousness and death. Multiple contributors describe spice as having fundamentally changed the nature of drug use in women's prisons over the past decade.

Spin – A cell search. My pad got spun means an officer searched the cell, typically looking for contraband, unauthorised items or evidence of rule-breaking.

Swinging a line – The practice of passing items between cells using an improvised cord made from clothing, bedding or other materials. Used to transfer drugs, notes, phones or other prohibited items between adjacent or nearby cells.

T

Throwers – Individuals, typically based outside the prison perimeter, who specialise in throwing packages of contraband over prison walls or fences. Neah Tuohy describes the role as essentially professional, requiring skill, local knowledge and practice.

Top dog – The dominant prisoner on a wing. In the women's estate this role is often more socially complex than the equivalent in male prisons, involving the management of relationships, information and informal welfare as well as the exercise of authority.

V

VP – Vulnerable Prisoner. A prisoner who requires separation from the general population for their own safety, whether because of the nature of their offence, a threat from other prisoners, or their own mental or physical vulnerability. High-profile prisoners such as those described in this book are frequently managed as VPs on arrival.

Acknowledgements

Thank you to the wonderful Ciara Lloyd, Publishing Director at Bonnier Books UK, for her sharp eye, savvy, warmth and patience. Always an immense pleasure to work together. Thanks as always to our marvellous agents, Matt Cole and Diane Banks at Northbank Talent Management.

We have felt as held as always by family and friends during the writing of this book, but particularly Valentina Serra, Alison Berridge, Stuart Estell, Gemma Heron-Brown, Dr Bhanu Williams and Dr Matt Williams. A special shout-out to a quartet of cool, powerful women who have always supported these books: Natalie Assor, Sam Maley, Rosanne Oppenheimer and Debbie Wisnia. Two remarkable women have offered Emma support and inspiration since school: Dr Amanda Holton and Professor Jane Kingsley-Smith.

Thanks to Emma's truly amazing father, Roger, for

his care and attention, not just with this book but with every book and every facet of his children and grandchildren's lives.

Most of all, thank you to the remarkable women and men who contributed to this book with authenticity, honesty, bravery and love.